中央高校基本科研业务费专项资金资助出版
（编号：N142303010）

不确定环境下的进入—退出决策

Entry-exit Decisions under Uncertainty

张永超　　张　娜　　著

东北大学出版社
·沈阳·

图书在版编目（CIP）数据

不确定环境下的进入—退出决策 = Entry-exit Decisions under Uncertainty: 英文 / 张永超，张娜著. —沈阳：东北大学出版社，2016.9
ISBN 978-7-5517-1413-6

Ⅰ. ①不… Ⅱ. ①张… ②张… Ⅲ. ①产品成本—研究—英文 ②价格—研究—英文 Ⅳ. ①F275.3 ②F014.3

中国版本图书馆 CIP 数据核字（2016）第 235817 号

出 版 者：东北大学出版社
地址：沈阳市和平区文化路三号巷 11 号
邮编：110819
电话：024-83687331（市场部） 83680267（社务部）
传真：024-83680180（市场部） 83687332（社务部）
网址：http：//www.neupress.com
E-mail：neuph@neupress.com
印 刷 者：沈阳中科印刷有限责任公司
发 行 者：东北大学出版社
幅面尺寸：170mm×230mm
印　　张：7.75
字　　数：149 千字
出版时间：2016 年 9 月第 1 版
印刷时间：2016 年 9 月第 1 次印刷
责任编辑：刘乃义
责任校对：刘　莹
封面设计：刘江旸
责任出版：唐敏志

ISBN 978-7-5517-1413-6　　定　价：28.00 元

Preface

Entry-exit decisions apply to numerous practical problems. For example, when to extract oil and when to stop the extraction, when to issue a new policy and when to end it, and when to let a kind of product enter a market and when to let the product exit the market, etc. Therefore, entry-exit decision problems attract a lot of researchers.

There are three approaches to study entry-exit decisions, namely, real option, pure probability and optimal stopping. In this monograph, we appeal to optimal stopping to deal with entry-exit decisions. The main reasons are as follows. On the one hand, in the real option framework, the regularity of payoff functions is *a priori* assumed, while the optimal stopping approach intends to prove it. On the other hand, although the pure probability and optimal stopping approaches are both to solve a optimal stopping problem, we have to calculate density functions of some stopping times if applying the pure probability approach, which is not easy, whereas the optimal stopping one avoids such calculations.

We aim to obtain closed-form solutions of optimal entry-exit decisions for the cases: costs depending on underlying processes, implementation with delay, and underlying processes following geometric Lévy processes. In addition, we provide a complete theory for optimal stopping problems with regime switching, and use it to solve an exit problem.

Many thanks are due to Zheng You-quan and Zhou Qing-long for helpful conversations. The authors greatly appreciate the help with regard to LaTeX provided by Pan Jian-yu and Wan Fu-yong . The authors are also grateful to the editors of Northeastern University Press for their highly professional and excellent work.

The publication of the monograph is financed by the Fundamental Research Funds for the Central Universities (Grant No. N142303010).

Errors surely still remain and the authors would deeply appreciate readers' assistance concerning these.

Zhang Yong-chao
Qinhuangdao, Hebei
zhangyc@neuq.edu.cn

Zhang Na
Taiyuan, Shanxi
nazhang0804@163.com

Contents

Overview

Consider an investment as follows.

> A firm has an option to invest in a project as well as stop it. To start the project activity, the firm needs an initial investment cost to produce a single commodity at a running cost. For simplicity, let us assume that the firm produces one unit commodity per unit time when the project is active. Besides, it may also abandon the project at a terminal investment cost.

What time is optimal to enter the project and what time is optimal to exit the project? The above problem is the so-called "entry-exit decision" problem in literature.

Dixit[18] explored this problem under the framework of real option theory, assuming that the price process of one unit commodity obeys a geometric Brownian motion. He derived a system of ordinary differential equations by following a no arbitrage argument and then obtained a semi-closed solution. However, he did not prove the existence and uniqueness of the solution of the system before doing numerical analysis.

Shirakawa[40] showed a more explicit solution by employing pure probabilistic analysis under the same assumptions as Dixit's. In his discussions, density functions of some stopping times need to be calculated, which is not an easy thing. Kongsted[30] established a general deterministic limit that corresponds to Dixit's model of entry-exit decisions under uncertainty.

Dixit[18] considered some extensions without explicit calculations. Tsekrekos[43] intensively studied one of these extensions that the price process follows a geometric mean-reverting process. Another mean-reverting process used in literature is the exponential Ornstein-Uhlenbeck process. Under the assumption that the price process satisfies an exponential Ornstein-Uhlenbeck process, Levendorskiĭ[31] dealt with an entry decision problem and an exit decision problem after discussing perpetual American options.

Duckworth and Zervos[19] and Sødal[41] modeled the price process via general autonomous Itô diffusions. Duckworth and Zervos[19] allowed running payoff functions to take nonlinear forms and then addressed the problem from the programming approach. However, in order to get explicit solutions, they assumed that the initial investment cost and terminal investment cost are some constants. Sødal[41] used a discount factor approach to investment to analyse entry-exit decisions. For obtaining explicit solutions, both Duckworth and Zervos[19] and Sødal[41] assumed that the price process follows a geometric Brownian motion.

Boyarchenko and Levendorskiĭ[6] studied entry decision problems and exit decision decision problems in general Lévy process settings via the real option approach. They adopted Wiener-Hopf factorization, which is a perfect result in the probability theory, in their discussions.

Under the assumption that the price process satisfies a geometric Brownian motion whose mean and variance switch between a finite number of regimes, Hainaut[26] investigated entry-exit decisions and obtained a semi-closed solution subject to determinate times.

The references mentioned above mainly focus on different price processes. There are some other directions of extending Dixit's model, for instance, uncertain costs, multiple entry-exit decisions, investment lags, etc.

Pindyck[37] derived an entry decision rule for an irreversible investment subject to an uncertain running cost (without any initial investment cost and terminal investment cost), assuming that the value of the project is known with certainty. In some sense, Choi and Lee[13] established a more general model than Pindyck's. Then, through the real option approach, they provided a semi-closed solution of entry-exit decisions.

Brekke and Øksendal[7] explored multiple entry-exit decisions via solving an impulse control problem. They obtained an explicit solution by assuming that the price process obeys a geometric Brownian motion and the costs are some constants. Johnson and Zervos[27] intensively studied multiple entry-exit decisions. They allowed running payoff functions to take nonlinear forms. However, in order to get explicit solutions, they assumed that the initial investment cost and terminal investment cost are some constants and the price process satisfies a geometric Brownian motion.

Under the same provisos as Dixit's, investment lags were considered by Bar-Ilan and Strange[3]. They derived a system of ordinary differential equations by a no arbitrage argument and then obtained a semi-closed solution. However, they did not prove the existence and uniqueness of the solution of the system before showing numerical analysis. Applying the probabilistic approach to the entry-exit decisions with the Parisian implementation delay, Costeniuc *et al.*[15] presented an analytic solution to the optimal starting and stopping levels.

In this monograph, which is based on [45, Chapter 3] and [46–49], we study entry-exit decisions from the perspective of optimal stopping, and provide explicit solutions to them. Chapter 1 disposes of entry-exit decisions with linear costs which may be viewed as a class of uncertain costs. Implementation delay is examined in Chapter 2. In Chapter 3, we deal with the cases where underlying precesses obey geometric Lévy processes. The last chapter attends to optimal stopping problems with regime switching. We appeal to the verification argument, viscosity solution technique and Wiener-Hopf factorization to solve optimal stopping problems.

1
Entry-exit decisions with linear costs

Summary: Instead of assuming that costs are constant in classical research, we assume that they are linear with respect to the price of the commodity produced by a project. Under this assumption, we obtain a condition which guarantees that investing in the project is worthless; additionally, the project may be terminated when the commodity price is greater than a certain value. In contrast, there are no such results provided that the costs are constant. Moreover, we provide an explicit solution of entry-exit decisions if the project is worthy to be invested in.

1.1 Introduction

We do not assume that costs are constants as in classical literature, but that they are some linear functions of the commodity price. Therefore, each cost consists of two parts. One part is fixed, and the other part is proportional to the commodity price. Consequently, the costs are uncertain. As usual, we accept that the price process follows a geometric Brownian motion and, for some integrability reason, the discount rate is greater than the drift of the geometric Brownian motion.

If the costs are constant, there is always a certain time at which the firm should enter the project. However, if the costs are some linear functions of the commodity price, we obtain a condition which guarantees that the firm should never enter the project (Theorem 1.5.1 or the conclusion ① of Theorem 1.5.10). We also obtain an explicit solution of entry-exit decisions provided that the project is worthy to be invested in (the conclusions ② and ③ of Theorem 1.5.10).

Assume that the firm has already entered the project. If the costs are constant, under some provisos, the firm should exit the project when the price is less than a certain value. However, there is another possibility if the costs are linear with respect to the commodity price. That is, under some assumptions, the firm may exit the project so as to get the maximal expected profit when the price is greater than a certain value (Theorem 1.4.5 and Theorem 1.4.7). As a comparison, there is no such a result in the case that the costs are constant.

The rest of the chapter is organized as follows. In Section 1.2, we introduce an elementary theory of optimal stopping problems. In Section 1.3, the model is described in detail. In Section 1.4, we offer an optimal exit time premised on the assumption that the firm has already activated the project. In Section 1.5, we obtain an optimal entry-exit decision as to when the firm enters the project and when exits the project. Some conclusions are drawn in Section 1.6.

1.2 An elementary introduction to optimal stopping problems

Let us turn our attention to more general optimal stopping problems.

The materials in this section are mainly taken from [35, pp. 27–28] and [39, pp. 231–235]. Let $(\Omega, \mathscr{F}, \{\mathscr{F}_t\}_{t\geq 0}, \mathbb{P})$ be a filtered probability space. We assume that $\{\mathscr{F}_t\}_{t\geq 0}$ satisfies the usual conditions and $\mathscr{F}_0$ is the completion of $\{\emptyset, \Omega\}$. Let $B = (B(t), t \geq 0)$ be a d-dimensional standard Brownian motion.

Fix an open set $\mathcal{S} \subset \mathbb{R}^{1+n}$ and let $Y = (Y(t), t \geq 0)$ be a diffusion in $\mathbb{R}^n$ given by

$$\mathrm{d}Y(t) = \alpha(t, Y(t))\mathrm{d}t + \beta(t, Y(t))\mathrm{d}B(t), \quad Y(0) = y,$$

where $\alpha : \overline{\mathbb{R}^+} \times \mathbb{R}^n \to \mathbb{R}^n$ and $\beta : \overline{\mathbb{R}^+} \times \mathbb{R}^n \to \mathbb{R}^{n\times d}$ are given two functions such that a unique strong solution Y exists.

Define $T_{\mathcal{S}} := \inf\{t > 0 : (t, Y(t)) \notin \mathcal{S}\}$ and let $\mathcal{T}$ denote the set of all stopping times $\tau \leq T_{\mathcal{S}}$.

For any $\tau \in \mathcal{T}$ and $y \in \mathbb{R}^n$, we define

$$J^{\tau}(y) := \mathbb{E}\left[\int_0^{\tau} f(t, Y(t))\mathrm{d}t + g(\tau, Y(\tau)) \cdot \mathbf{1}_{\{\tau<\infty\}} \middle| Y(0) = y\right],$$

where $f : \overline{\mathbb{R}^+} \times \mathbb{R}^n \to \mathbb{R}$ and $g : \overline{\mathbb{R}^+} \times \mathbb{R}^n \to \mathbb{R}$ are two functions such that the expectation $J^{\tau}(y)$ exits.

Then the general optimal stopping problem is described as follows.

(1.2.1) Find $\hat{J}(y)$ and $\tau^* \in \mathcal{T}$ such that $\hat{J}(y) = \sup_{\tau\in\mathcal{T}} J^{\tau}(y) = J^{\tau^*}(y)$.

Now we give a procedure for solving the optimal stopping problem (1.2.1).

(1) Find a function ϕ defined on $\overline{\mathcal{S}}$ and an open set $D \subset \mathcal{S} \cap ((0, +\infty) \times \mathbb{R}^n)$ such that the following properties hold.

(1.a) The function ϕ is C^1 in $\mathcal{S}$.

(1.b) The equality $\frac{\partial}{\partial t}\phi(t, y) + \mathcal{L}\phi(t, y) + f(t, y) = 0$ holds in D, where $\mathcal{L}$ is the infinitesimal generator of the diffusion Y. Moreover, for any $(t, y) \in \partial D$ with $t > 0$, we have $\phi(t, y) = g(t, y)$.

(1.c) The inequality $\phi \geq g$ holds in $\mathcal{S}$, and the inequality $\phi > g$ holds in D.

(1.d) The inequality $\frac{\partial}{\partial t}\phi(t, y) + \mathcal{L}\phi(t, y) + f(t, y) \leq 0$ holds in $\mathcal{S} \setminus \overline{D}$.

(2) Verify that the stopping time $\tau^* := \inf\{t : t > 0, (t, Y(t)) \notin D\}$ is an optimal stopping time and the function $\hat{J}$ in (1.2.1) is given by $\hat{J}(y) = \phi(0, y)$.

Remark 1.2.1 The above procedure is a modification of that in [39, pp. 234–235] or [35, p. 29, Theorem 2.2].

1.3 The model

Let $B(t)$ be a one dimensional standard Brownian motion, which denotes uncertainty in a market, defined on a filtered probability space $(\Omega, \mathscr{F}, \{\mathscr{F}_t\}_{t\geq 0}, \mathbb{P})$. Here, $\{\mathscr{F}_t\}_{t\geq 0}$ satisfies the usual conditions and $\mathscr{F}_0$ is the completion of $\{\emptyset, \Omega\}$.

We assume that the price process P follows

$$dP(t) = \mu P(t)dt + \sigma P(t)dB(t), \text{ and } P(0) > 0, \tag{1.3.1}$$

where $\mu \in \mathbb{R}$, and $\sigma > 0$.

Applying Itô's formula, we deduce that the solution of the equation (1.3.1) is

$$P(t) = P(0)\exp\left[\left(\mu - \frac{1}{2}\sigma^2\right)t + \sigma B(t)\right]. \tag{1.3.2}$$

The firm is risk neutral. Moreover, the running cost C, the initial investment cost K_I and the terminal investment cost K_O are taken the following forms:

$$\begin{aligned} C(p) &= c_1 p + c_0, \\ K_I(p) &= k_1 p + k_0, \\ K_O(p) &= l_1 p + l_0, \end{aligned}$$

respectively. Here, c_i, k_i and l_i are some constants, $i = 0, 1$, such that $c_0 \geq 0$, $k_0 \geq 0$, $k_0 + l_0 \geq 0$ and $k_1 + l_1 \geq 0$.

To answer the questions—what time is optimal to enter (exit) the project, we will solve the optimal problem

$$\begin{aligned} \hat{J}_{IO}(p) := \sup_{0 \leq \tau_I \leq \tau_O} \mathbb{E}\bigg[\int_{\tau_I}^{\tau_O} & \exp(-rt)(P(t) - c_1 P(t) - c_0)dt - \\ & \exp(-r\tau_I)\left(k_1 P(\tau_I) + k_0\right) - \\ & \exp(-r\tau_O)\left(l_1 P(\tau_O) + l_0\right) \big| P(0) = p\bigg], \end{aligned} \tag{1.3.3}$$

where τ_I and τ_O are stopping times, and r is the discount rate such that $r > 0$. As usual (for some integrability reason), we assume that $r > \mu$. We call the stopping times τ_I and τ_O entry times and exit times, respectively. We refer to the function $\hat{J}_{IO}$ as the maximal expected present value of the project.

1.4 An optimal exit time

In this section, we assume that the firm has already activated the project. So we may ask at what time the firm should stop the project. This problem can be solved by considering the optimal problem

$$\begin{aligned}(1.4.1)\qquad \hat{J}_O(p) := \sup_{0\le\tau_O} \mathbb{E}\Bigg[\int_0^{\tau_O} &\exp(-rt)((1-c_1)P(t)-c_0)\mathrm{d}t - \\ &\exp(-r\tau_O)(l_1P(\tau_O)+l_0)|\, P(0)=p\Bigg].\end{aligned}$$

We want to find a stopping time τ_O^* (called an optimal exit time) such that

$$\begin{aligned}\hat{J}_O(p) =\mathbb{E}\Bigg[\int_0^{\tau_O^*} &\exp(-rt)((1-c_1)P(t)-c_0)\mathrm{d}t - \\ &\exp(-r\tau_O^*)(l_1P(\tau_O^*)+l_0)|\, P(0)=p\Bigg],\end{aligned}$$

and an explicit expression of $\hat{J}_O$.

The following lemma is useful in our discussions.

Lemma 1.4.1 *The family of random variables* $\{\exp\left[(\mu-r-\sigma^2/2)\tau+\sigma B(\tau)\right]:\tau\in\mathcal{T}\}$ *is uniformly integrable, where* $\mathcal{T}$ *is the collection of all stopping times.*

Proof. Taking a real number α such that $1<\alpha<1+2(r-\mu)/\sigma^2$, we have

$$(1.4.2)\qquad \alpha\left(\mu-r-\frac{\sigma^2}{2}\right)+\frac{\alpha^2\sigma^2}{2}<0.$$

Define $X(t) := \exp\left[(\mu-r-\sigma^2/2)t+\sigma B(t)\right]$ for any $t\ge 0$. Then for any $s<t$, we find that

$$\begin{aligned}\mathbb{E}\left[X(t)^\alpha|\mathscr{F}_s\right] &= \exp\left[\alpha\left(\mu-r-\frac{\sigma^2}{2}\right)t+\frac{\alpha^2\sigma^2}{2}(t-s)+\alpha\sigma B(s)\right] \\ &\le X(s)^\alpha,\end{aligned}$$

where we have used the fact that the process

$$\left(\exp\left(-\frac{\alpha^2\sigma^2}{2}t+\alpha\sigma B(t)\right),t\ge 0\right)$$

is a martingale (see [1, p. 288, Corollary 5.2.2]) for the equality and (1.4.2) for the inequality.

Thus $(X(t)^\alpha, t\ge 0)$ is a supermartingale with a last element 0.

Then from Doob's optional sampling theorem (see [28, p. 19, Theorem 3.22] or [38, p. 9, Theorem 16]), it follows that

$$\mathbb{E}\left[X(\tau)^{\alpha}\right] \le X(0)^{\alpha} = 1,$$

for any stopping time τ.

Therefore, according to [38, pp. 8–9, Theorem 11], the family of random variables $\left\{\exp\left[(\mu - r - \sigma^2/2)\tau + \sigma B(\tau)\right] : \tau \in \mathcal{T}\right\}$ is uniformly integrable. □

Theorem 1.4.2 *Assume that one of the following conditions*

① $l_1(r-\mu) - c_1 > -1$ *and* $c_0 \le r l_0$,

② $l_1(r-\mu) - c_1 = -1$ *and* $c_0 < r l_0$

holds. Then the optimal exit time τ_O^* *is given by* $\tau_O^* = +\infty$ *a.s., i.e., the firm should never exit the project. Furthermore, the function* $\hat{J}_O$ *in* (1.4.1) *is given by* $\hat{J}_O(p) = \dfrac{1-c_1}{r-\mu}p - \dfrac{c_0}{r}$.

Proof. (1) Define an operator $\mathcal{L}$ by

$$\mathcal{L}\zeta(t,p) = \frac{\partial \zeta}{\partial t} + \mu p \frac{\partial \zeta}{\partial p} + \frac{1}{2}\sigma^2 p^2 \frac{\partial^2 \zeta}{\partial p^2}. \tag{1.4.3}$$

(Warning! Here, $\mathcal{L}$ is not the infinitesimal generator of the price process P.)

For any $(s,p) \in \overline{\mathbb{R}^+} \times (0,+\infty)$, set $f(s,p) := \exp(-rs)\left[(1-c_1)p - c_0\right]$ and $g(s,p) := -\exp(-rs)(l_1 p + l_0)$. Then, via a direct calculation, we find that

$$\mathcal{L}g(s,p) > -f(s,p).$$

(2) By Itô's formula, it follows that for $s \le t$

(1.4.4)

$$g(t,P(t)) = g(s,P(s)) + \int_s^t \mathcal{L}g(u,P(u))\mathrm{d}s + \int_s^t \frac{\partial g}{\partial p}(u,P(u))\sigma P(u)\mathrm{d}B(u).$$

For a nonnegative number s, define a sequence of stopping times $(R_k(s), k \in \mathbb{N})$ by $R_k(s) := \inf\{t : t > s, P(t) > k\}$. Next, for a stopping time τ, define a sequence of stopping times $(\tau_k(s), k \in \mathbb{N})$ by $\tau_k(s) := (\tau \wedge k \wedge R_k(s)) \vee s$. Then using the optional sampling theorem (see [32, p. 53, Theorem 1.86] or [38, p. 10, Theorem 17]), we have

$$\mathbb{E}\left[\int_s^{\tau_k(s)} \frac{\partial g}{\partial p}(u,P(u))\sigma P(u)\mathrm{d}B(u) \,\middle|\, P(s) = p\right] = 0. \tag{1.4.5}$$

Therefore, combining (1.4.4) and (1.4.5), it follows that for any stopping time $\tau \geq s$

(1.4.6)

$$\mathbb{E}\left[g(\tau_k, P(\tau_k))\middle| P(s)=p\right] = g(s,p) + \mathbb{E}\left[\int_s^{\tau_k(s)} \mathcal{L}g(t,P(t))\mathrm{d}t\middle| P(s)=p\right].$$

Note that

$$\begin{aligned}&\lim_{T\to+\infty} \mathbb{E}\left[\int_0^T \exp(-rt)P(t)\mathrm{d}t\middle| P(0)=p\right]\\ &=\lim_{T\to+\infty}\int_0^T \exp(-rt)p\exp(\mu t)\mathrm{d}t \qquad (1.4.7)\\ &=\frac{p}{r-\mu},\end{aligned}$$

where we have used the fact that the process

$$\left(\exp\left(-\frac{1}{2}\sigma^2 t + \sigma B(t)\right), t \geq 0\right)$$

is a martingale (see [1, p. 288, Corollary 5.2.2]) for the first equality.

Taking limits in (1.4.6), we have

$$\mathbb{E}\left[g(\tau, P(\tau))\middle| P(s)=p\right] = g(s,p) + \mathbb{E}\left[\int_s^{\tau} \mathcal{L}g(t,P(t))\mathrm{d}t\middle| P(s)=p\right],$$

where we have used Lemma 1.4.1 for the left side and (1.4.7) for the right side.

Furthermore, by noting that $\mathcal{L}g(s,p) > -f(s,p)$, we find that

$$\mathbb{E}\left[g(\tau, P(\tau))\middle| P(s)=p\right] > g(s,p) - \mathbb{E}\left[\int_s^{\tau} f(t,P(t))\mathrm{d}t\middle| P(s)=p\right],$$

which means that

$$\begin{aligned}-\exp(-rs)(l_1p+l_0) < \mathbb{E}\Bigg[&\int_s^{\tau}\exp(-rt)((1-c_1)P(t)-c_0)\mathrm{d}t-\\ &\exp(-r\tau)(l_1P(\tau)+l_0)\Big| P(s)=p\Bigg]\\ \leq{}& \Phi(s,p),\end{aligned}$$

where the function Φ is defined by

$$\Phi(s,p) = \sup_{s \le \tau_O} \mathbb{E}\Bigg[\int_s^{\tau_O} \exp(-rt)((1-c_1)P(t)-c_0)\mathrm{d}t - \exp(-r\tau_O)(l_1 P(\tau_O)+l_0)\Big|\, P(s)=p\Bigg].$$

Hence any $(s,p) \in \overline{\mathbb{R}^+} \times (0,+\infty)$ is in the so-called *optimal continuation region* $\{(s,p) : (s,p) \in \overline{\mathbb{R}^+} \times (0,+\infty)$ and $-\exp(-rs)(l_1 p + l_0) < \Phi(s,p)\}$ (see [39, p. 232]). This implies $\tau_O^* = +\infty$ a.s., and $\hat{J}_O(p) = \dfrac{1-c_1}{r-\mu}p - \dfrac{c_0}{r}$ by some similar calculations to (1.4.7). □

Theorem 1.4.3 *Assume that* $l_1(r-\mu) - c_1 \le -1$ *and* $c_0 \ge r l_0$. *Then the optimal exit time* τ_O^* *is given by* $\tau_O^* = 0$ *a.s., i.e., the firm should immediately exit the project. In addition, the function* $\hat{J}_O$ *in* (1.4.1) *is given by* $\hat{J}_O(p) = -l_1 p - l_0$.

Proof. In this case, we have

$$\mathcal{L}g(s,p) \le -f(s,p).$$

(For the definitions of $\mathcal{L}$, f and g, please see Step 1 of the proof of Theorem 1.4.2.)

By a similar method to that in Step 2 of the proof of Theorem 1.4.2, it follows that

$$\begin{aligned}\mathbb{E}\left[g(\tau,P(\tau))\,|\,P(0)=p\right] &= g(0,p) + \mathbb{E}\left[\int_0^{\tau} \mathcal{L}g(t,P(t))\mathrm{d}t\,\Big|\, P(0)=p\right] \\ &\le -l_1 p - l_0 - \mathbb{E}\left[\int_0^{\tau} f(t,P(t))\mathrm{d}t\,\Big|\, P(0)=p\right],\end{aligned}$$

for any stopping time τ.

Therefore,

$$\mathbb{E}\left[\int_0^{\tau} f(t,P(t))\mathrm{d}t + g(\tau,P(\tau))\,\Big|\, P(0)=p\right] \le -l_1 p - l_0,$$

which implies that the optimal exit time τ_O^* is given by $\tau_O^* = 0$ a.s. and the function $\hat{J}_O$ in (1.4.1) is given by $\hat{J}_O(p) = -l_1 p - l_0$. □

Now we consider the case that $l_1(r-\mu)-c_1>-1$ and $c_0>rl_0$. The following lemma is needed in discussing this case.

Lemma 1.4.4 *The function $\hat{J}_O(\cdot)$ in (1.4.1) is Lipschitz continuous on $[0,+\infty)$. Consequently, $\hat{J}_O(\cdot)$ is a linear growth function.*

Proof. By (1.4.7), we have

$$\mathbb{E}\left[\int_0^{+\infty}\exp(-rt)P(t)\mathrm{d}t\,\middle|\,P(0)=p\right]=\frac{p}{r-\mu}.$$

Repeating the proof of Lemma 1.4.1, we find that

$$\mathbb{E}\left[\exp(-r\tau)P(\tau)\,|\,P(0)=p\right]\le p$$

for any stopping time τ.

Therefore, by the definition of the function $\hat{J}_O(\cdot)$ and (1.3.2), it follows that, for any p_1, $p_2\in[0,+\infty)$,

$$|\hat{J}_O(p_1)-\hat{J}_O(p_2)|\le\left(\frac{1-c_1}{r-\mu}+l_1\right)|p_1-p_2|,$$

which implies that the function $\hat{J}_O(\cdot)$ is Lipschitz continuous on $[0,+\infty)$. □

The following observations will be used in the proofs of Theorems 1.4.5, 1.4.7, 1.5.4 and 1.5.7. Let λ_1 and λ_2 be the solutions of the quadratic equation

$$-r+\mu\lambda+\frac{1}{2}\sigma^2\lambda(\lambda-1)=0$$

with $\lambda_1<\lambda_2$. Then we have $\lambda_1<0$ and $\lambda_2>1$. In addition, $\lambda_1>r/\mu$ if $\mu<0$, and $\lambda_2<r/\mu$ if $\mu>0$.

Theorem 1.4.5 *Assume that $l_1(r-\mu)-c_1>-1$ and $c_0>rl_0$. Then the function $\hat{J}_O$ in (1.4.1) is given by*

$$\hat{J}_O(p)=\begin{cases}A_1p^{\lambda_1}+\dfrac{1-c_1}{r-\mu}p-\dfrac{c_0}{r}, & \text{if } p>p_O,\\[2mm] -l_1p-l_0, & \text{if } p\le p_O,\end{cases}$$

where

$$p_O=\frac{\lambda_1}{\lambda_1-1}\times\frac{r-\mu}{1-c_1+l_1(r-\mu)}\left(\frac{c_0}{r}-l_0\right),$$

and

$$A_1 = \frac{1 - c_1 + l_1(r - \mu)}{\lambda_1(\mu - r)} {p_O}^{1-\lambda_1}.$$

In addition, the optimal exit time τ_O^* *is given by*

$$\tau_O^* = \inf\{t : t > 0 \text{ and } P(t) \le p_O\}.$$

Before proving Theorem 1.4.5, we would like to explain the economic meaning of it. Assume that the firm has already activated the project. If $l_1(r - \mu) - c_1 > -1$ and $c_0 > rl_0$, the firm should exit the project when the commodity price is less than or equal to p_O, and the maximal expected present value of the project is given by $\hat{J}_O$ in Theorem 1.4.5.

Proof of Theorem 1.4.5. (1) Recall the definition of the operator $\mathcal{L}$ [see (1.4.3)],

$$\mathcal{L}\zeta(t,p) = \frac{\partial \zeta}{\partial t} + \mu p \frac{\partial \zeta}{\partial p} + \frac{1}{2}\sigma^2 p^2 \frac{\partial^2 \zeta}{\partial p^2}.$$

We make an *ansatz*

(1.4.8)

$$\phi(t,p) = \begin{cases} \exp(-rt)\left(A_1 p^{\lambda} + A_2 p + A_3\right) \text{ in } D_O := (0,+\infty) \times (p_O, +\infty), \\ -\exp(-rt)(l_1 p + l_0) \text{ on } (0,+\infty) \times [0, p_O]. \end{cases}$$

Then by (1.b) in the procedure for solving optimal stopping problems (see Section 1.2), we have

$$-r\exp(-rt)\left(A_1 p^{\lambda} + A_2 p + A_3\right) + \mu \exp(-rt) p \left(A_1 \lambda p^{\lambda-1} + A_2\right) +$$
$$\frac{1}{2}\sigma^2 \exp(-rt) p^2 A_1 \lambda(\lambda - 1) p^{\lambda-2} + \exp(-rt)\left[(1 - c_1)p - c_0\right] = 0,$$

by which we require

$$\begin{cases} -r + \mu\lambda + \frac{1}{2}\sigma^2\lambda(\lambda - 1) = 0 \\ -rA_2 + \mu A_2 + 1 - c_1 = 0 \\ -rA_3 - c_0 = 0. \end{cases}$$

Therefore, we have $\lambda = \lambda_1$ or $\lambda = \lambda_2$, $A_2 = \dfrac{1 - c_1}{r - \mu}$ and $A_3 = -\dfrac{c_0}{r}$. Since the function $\hat{J}_O(\cdot)$ is a linear growth function by Lemma 1.4.4, we must choose $\lambda = \lambda_1$.

By (1.a) in the procedure for solving optimal stopping problems, we have

$$(1.4.9)\qquad \begin{cases} A_1 p_O^{\lambda_1} + \dfrac{1-c_1}{r-\mu} p_O - \dfrac{c_0}{r} = -l_1 p_O - l_0 \\ \lambda_1 A_1 p_O^{\lambda_1 - 1} + \dfrac{1-c_1}{r-\mu} = -l_1, \end{cases}$$

from which we obtain

$$p_O = \frac{\lambda_1}{\lambda_1 - 1} \times \frac{r-\mu}{1-c_1+l_1(r-\mu)} \left(\frac{c_0}{r} - l_0\right)$$

and

$$A_1 = \frac{1-c_1+l_1(r-\mu)}{\lambda_1(\mu - r)} p_O{}^{1-\lambda_1}.$$

Now we have seen that the function (1.4.8) satisfies (1.a) and (1.b). We have to check (1.c) and (1.d).

(2) For (1.c) we only have to check that the inequality $\phi(t,p) > -\exp(-rt)\times (l_1 p + l_0)$ holds in D_O.

Define a function $h(p) := A_1 p^{\lambda_1} + \dfrac{1-c_1}{r-\mu} p - \dfrac{c_0}{r} + l_1 p + l_0$. Then

$$h'(p) = \left[1 - \left(\frac{p}{p_O}\right)^{\lambda_1 - 1}\right] \frac{1-c_1+l_1(r-\mu)}{r-\mu} > 0$$

in $(p_O, +\infty)$. Thus the function $h(\cdot)$ is strictly monotone increasing in $(p_O, +\infty)$. On the other hand, we have $h(p_O) = 0$ by the construction of (1.4.8) [see the first equation of (1.4.9)]. Therefore, $A_1 p^{\lambda_1} + \dfrac{1-c_1}{r-\mu} p - \dfrac{c_0}{r} > -l_1 p - l_0$ for $p \in (p_O, +\infty)$, from which we see that the inequality $\phi(t,p) > -\exp(-rt)(l_1 p + l_0)$ holds in D_O.

(3) For (1.d) we only have to check that the inequality $\mathcal{L}\phi(t,p) + f(t,p) \le 0$ holds in $(0,+\infty) \times (0, p_O)$, where $f(t,p) := \exp(-rt)[(1-c_1)p - c_0]$.

Note that

$$(1.4.10)\qquad \frac{1}{\lambda_1} < \frac{\mu}{r}.$$

Combining (1.4.10) and $c_0 > r l_0$, we have

$$[1 - c_1 + l_1(r-\mu)] p_O = \frac{\lambda_1}{\lambda_1 - 1}(r-\mu)\left(\frac{c_0}{r} - l_0\right) < c_0 - r l_0.$$

Hence for any $(t,p) \in (0,+\infty) \times (0,p_O)$,

$$\begin{aligned}\mathcal{L}\phi(t,p) + f(t,p) &= \exp(-rt)\left\{[1-c_1+l_1(r-\mu)]p + rl_0 - c_0\right\} \\ &< \exp(-rt)\left\{[1-c_1+l_1(r-\mu)]p_O + rl_0 - c_0\right\} < 0.\end{aligned}$$

(4) We will prove $\hat{J}_O(p) = \phi(0,p)$ and $\tau_O^* = \inf\{t : t > 0 \text{ and } P(t) \le p_O\}$ directly in the following two steps.

Define a function $w(p)$ by

$$w(p) := \begin{cases} A_1 p^{\lambda_1} + \dfrac{1-c_1}{r-\mu}p - \dfrac{c_0}{r}, & \text{if } p > p_O, \\ -l_1 p - l_0, & \text{if } p \le p_O. \end{cases}$$

Then

$$w''(p) = \begin{cases} A_1\lambda_1(\lambda_1 - 1)p^{\lambda_1}, & \text{if } p > p_O, \\ 0, & \text{if } p < p_O. \end{cases}$$

Thus $w''(p) \ge 0$ except for $p = p_O$. However, the function $w(p)$ is continuous on $\mathbb{R}$. It follows that $w(p)$ is convex.

Therefore, by Meyer-Itô formula (see [38, p. 218, Theorem 70]), we have

$$\phi(t,P(t)) = \phi(0,P(0)) + \int_0^t \mathcal{L}\phi(s,P(s))\mathrm{d}s + \int_0^t \frac{\partial\phi}{\partial p}(s,P(s))\sigma P(s)\mathrm{d}B(s) + \frac{1}{2}L_t(p_O)\left(\frac{\partial\phi}{\partial p}(t,{p_O}^+) - \frac{\partial\phi}{\partial p}(t,{p_O}^-)\right),$$

where $L_t(p_O)$ is P's local time at p_O.

Note that $\dfrac{\partial\phi}{\partial p}(t,{p_O}^+) - \dfrac{\partial\phi}{\partial p}(t,{p_O}^-) = 0$ by the construction of the function (1.4.8) [see the second equation of (1.4.9)]. The following identity holds,

(1.4.11)
$$\phi(t,P(t)) = \phi(0,P(0)) + \int_0^t \mathcal{L}\phi(s,P(s))\mathrm{d}s + \int_0^t \frac{\partial\phi}{\partial p}(s,P(s))\sigma P(s)\mathrm{d}B(s).$$

Define a sequence of stopping times $(S_k, k \in \mathbb{N})$ by $S_k := \inf\{t : t > 0, P(t) > k\}$. Next, for a stopping time τ, define a sequence of stopping times $(\tau_k, k \in \mathbb{N})$ by $\tau_k := \tau \wedge k \wedge S_k$. Then using the optional sampling theorem (see [32, p. 53, Theorem 1.86] or [38, p. 10, Theorem 17]), we have

$$\mathbb{E}\left[\int_0^{\tau_k} \frac{\partial\phi}{\partial p}(s,P(s))\sigma P(s)\mathrm{d}B(s)\,\middle|\, P(0) = p\right] = 0. \tag{1.4.12}$$

Combining (1.4.11) and (1.4.12) yields

(1.4.13)
$$\mathbb{E}\left[\phi(\tau_k, P(\tau_k))\middle| P(0)=p\right] = \phi(0,p) + \mathbb{E}\left[\int_0^{\tau_k} \mathcal{L}\phi(s, P(s))\mathrm{d}s \middle| P(0)=p\right].$$

Note that $\phi(t,p) \geq -\exp(-rt)(l_1 p + l_0)$ by Step 2 and that $\mathcal{L}\phi(t,p) \leq -\exp(-rt)[(1-c_1)p - c_0]$ by Step 3. It follows from (1.4.13) that

$$\begin{aligned} &\mathbb{E}\left[-\exp(-r\tau_k)(l_1 P(\tau_k) + l_0)\middle| P(0)=p\right] \\ &\leq \phi(0,p) - \mathbb{E}\left[\int_0^{\tau_k} \exp(-rs)((1-c_1)P(s) - c_0)\mathrm{d}s \middle| P(0)=p\right]. \end{aligned} \tag{1.4.14}$$

By some similar calculations to (1.4.7), we have

$$\mathbb{E}\left[\int_0^{+\infty} \exp(-rs)|(1-c_1)P(s) - C|\mathrm{d}s \middle| P(0)=p\right] < +\infty.$$

Therefore, by taking limits as $k \to +\infty$ in (1.4.14), we obtain that

$$\begin{aligned} \mathbb{E}\Bigg[&\int_0^{\tau} \exp(-rs)((1-c_1)P(s) - C)\mathrm{d}s - \\ &\exp(-r\tau)(l_1 P(\tau) + l_0)\Big| P(0)=p\Bigg] \leq \phi(0,p), \end{aligned} \tag{1.4.15}$$

where we have used Lemma 1.4.1.

(5) Take $\tau = \tau_O^*$ in the definition of τ_k. Then

$$\begin{aligned} &\mathbb{E}\left[\phi(\tau_k, P(\tau_k))\middle| P(0)=p\right] \\ &= \mathbb{E}\left[\phi(\tau_k, P(\tau_k))\mathbf{1}_{\{\tau_O^* \leq k\wedge S_k\}}\middle| P(0)=p\right] + \\ &\quad \mathbb{E}\left[\phi(\tau_k, P(\tau_k))\mathbf{1}_{\{\tau_O^* > k\wedge S_k\}}\middle| P(0)=p\right] \\ &= \mathbb{E}\left[-\exp(-r\tau_O^*)(l_1 P(\tau_O^*) + l_0)\mathbf{1}_{\{\tau_O^* \leq k\wedge S_k\}}\middle| P(0)=p\right] + \\ &\quad \mathbb{E}\left[\phi(k\wedge S_k, P(k\wedge S_k))\mathbf{1}_{\{\tau_O^* > k\wedge S_k\}}\middle| P(0)=p\right]. \end{aligned} \tag{1.4.16}$$

Now we estimate $\mathbb{E}\left[\phi(k\wedge S_k, P(k\wedge S_k))\mathbf{1}_{\{\tau_O^* > k\wedge S_k\}}\middle| P(0)=p\right]$ (the last term of (1.4.16)).

First, we estimate $\mathbb{E}\left[\exp\left(-r(k\wedge S_k)\right)P(k\wedge S_k)^{\lambda_1}\mathbf{1}_{\{\tau_O^*>k\wedge S_k\}}\middle| P(0)=p\right]$.

$$\begin{aligned}&\mathbb{E}\left[\exp\left(-r(k\wedge S_k)\right)P(k\wedge S_k)^{\lambda_1}\mathbf{1}_{\{\tau_O^*>k\wedge S_k\}}\middle| P(0)=p\right]\\ \le\ & p_O^{\lambda_1}\mathbb{E}\left[\exp\left(-r(k\wedge S_k)\right)\mathbf{1}_{\{\tau_O^*>k\wedge S_k\}}\middle| P(0)=p\right]\\ \le\ & p_O^{\lambda_1}\mathbb{E}\left[\exp\left(-r(k\wedge S_k)\right)\middle| P(0)=p\right].\end{aligned}\tag{1.4.17}$$

Second, we estimate $\mathbb{E}\left[\exp\left(-r(k\wedge S_k)\right)P(k\wedge S_k)\mathbf{1}_{\{\tau_O^*>k\wedge S_k\}}\middle| P(0)=p\right]$. According to [1, p. 288, Corollary 5.2.2], we define a martingale M by

$$M:=\left(P(0)\exp\left(-\frac{1}{2}\sigma^2t+\sigma B(t)\right),t\ge 0\right).$$

Then

$$M(t)=P(0)+\int_0^t\sigma M(s)\mathrm{d}B(s),$$

and, by the optional sampling theorem (see [32, p. 53, Theorem 1.86] or [38, p. 10, Theorem 17]),

$$\mathbb{E}\left[\int_0^{k\wedge S_k}\exp(-(r-\mu)(k\wedge S_k))\,\sigma M(s)\mathrm{d}B(s)\middle| P(0)=p\right]=0.\tag{1.4.18}$$

Thus

$$\begin{aligned}&\mathbb{E}\left[\exp\left(-r(k\wedge S_k)\right)P(k\wedge S_k)\mathbf{1}_{\{\tau_O^*>k\wedge S_k\}}\middle| P(0)=p\right]\\ =\ &\mathbb{E}\left[\exp\left(-(r-\mu)(k\wedge S_k)\right)M(k\wedge S_k)\mathbf{1}_{\{\tau_O^*>k\wedge S_k\}}\middle| P(0)=p\right]\\ \le\ &\mathbb{E}\left[\exp\left(-(r-\mu)(k\wedge S_k)\right)M(k\wedge S_k)\middle| P(0)=p\right]\\ =\ &p\,\mathbb{E}\left[\exp\left(-(r-\mu)(k\wedge S_k)\right)\middle| P(0)=p\right],\end{aligned}\tag{1.4.19}$$

where we have used (1.4.18) for the last equality.

Finally, the following inequality holds,

$$\mathbb{E}\left[\exp\left(-r(k\wedge S_k)\right)\mathbf{1}_{\{\tau_O^*>k\wedge S_k\}}\middle| P(0)=p\right]\le\mathbb{E}\left[\exp\left(-r(k\wedge S_k)\right)\middle| P(0)=p\right].\tag{1.4.20}$$

Therefore, by (1.4.17), (1.4.19), (1.4.20) and the definition of the function ϕ (see (1.4.8)), we have

$$\lim_{k\to+\infty}\mathbb{E}\left[\phi(\tau_k,P(\tau_k))\mathbf{1}_{\{\tau_O^*>k\wedge S_k\}}\middle| P(0)=p\right]=0.\tag{1.4.21}$$

Inserting (1.4.21) into (1.4.16), it follows that

$$\lim_{k\to+\infty} \mathbb{E}\left[\phi(\tau_k, P(\tau_k)) \middle| P(0)=p\right] = \mathbb{E}\left[-\exp(-r\tau_O^*)(l_1 P(\tau_O^*)+l_0) \middle| P(0)=p\right].$$

Note that $\mathcal{L}\phi(s,P(s)) = -\exp(-rs)[(1-c_1)P(s)-c_0]$ if $0<s<\tau_O^*$. Then, by taking limits as $k\to+\infty$ in (1.4.13), it follows that

$$\mathbb{E}\Bigg[\int_0^{\tau_O^*} \exp(-rs)((1-c_1)P(s)-c_0)\mathrm{d}s - \exp(-r\tau_O^*)(l_1 P(\tau_O^*)+l_0) \Big| P(0)=p\Bigg] = \phi(0,p). \tag{1.4.22}$$

Combining (1.4.15) and (1.4.22), we have proved that $\hat{J}_O(p) = \phi(0,p)$ and $\tau_O^* = \inf\{t : t>0 \text{ and } P(t)\le p_O\}$. □

Corollary 1.4.6 *The optimal exit trigger price p_O in Theorem 1.4.5 satisfies* $p_O < \dfrac{c_0 - rl_0}{1-c_1+l_1(r-\mu)}$.

Proof. See Step 3 of the proof of Theorem 1.4.5. □

Theorem 1.4.7 *Assume that $l_1(r-\mu)-c_1<-1$ and $c_0<rl_0$. Then the function $\hat{J}_O$ in (1.4.1) is given by*

$$\hat{J}_O(p) = \begin{cases} A_1 p^{\lambda_2} + \dfrac{1-c_1}{r-\mu}p - \dfrac{c_0}{r}, & \text{if } p<p_O, \\ -l_1 p - l_0, & \text{if } p \ge p_O, \end{cases}$$

where

$$p_O = \frac{\lambda_2}{\lambda_2-1}\times\frac{r-\mu}{1-c_1+l_1(r-\mu)}\left(\frac{c_0}{r}-l_0\right),$$

and

$$A_1 = \frac{1-c_1+l_1(r-\mu)}{\lambda_2(\mu-r)}p_O^{1-\lambda_2}.$$

In addition, the optimal exit time τ_O^* is given by

$$\tau_O^* = \inf\{t : t>0 \text{ and } P(t)\ge p_O\}.$$

Furthermore, the optimal exit trigger price p_O satisfies

$$p_O > \frac{c_0-rl_0}{1-c_1+l_1(r-\mu)}.$$

Proof. The proof is similar to that of Theorem 1.4.5. □

It is interesting to compare Theorem 1.4.5 with Theorem 1.4.7. The stopping region in Theorem 1.4.5 takes the form of $[0, p_O]$ while the stopping region in Theorem 1.4.7 takes the form of $[p_O, +\infty)$. Intuitively, if the parameter l_1 in Theorem 1.4.7 is negative enough, the firm can profit from exiting the project provided that the price is high enough.

1.5 An optimal entry-exit decision

In this section, we provide an optimal entry-exit decision, i.e., when the firm enters the project and when the firm exits the project. Meanwhile, we obtain an explicit expression of the maximal expected present value of the project.

Recall the definition of the maximal expected present value of the project [see (1.3.3)],

$$\hat{J}_{IO}(p) := \sup_{0\le\tau_I\le\tau_O} \mathbb{E}\Bigg[\int_{\tau_I}^{\tau_O} \exp(-rt)((1-c_1)P(t)-c_0)\mathrm{d}t - \exp(-r\tau_I)(k_1P(\tau_I)+k_0) - \exp(-r\tau_O)(l_1P(\tau_O)+l_0)\Big|\, P(0)=p\Bigg].$$

Define a function $J : [0, +\infty) \to \mathbb{R}$ by

$$J(p) := \sup_{0\le\tau_I} \mathbb{E}\left[\exp(-r\tau_I)\left(\hat{J}_O(P(\tau_I)) - k_1P(\tau_I) - k_0\right)\Big|\, P(0)=p\right]. \tag{1.5.1}$$

It will be proved in Theorem 1.5.10 that $J(p) = \hat{J}_{IO}(p)$ for $p \in [0, +\infty)$.

We want to find a stopping time τ_I^* (called an optimal entry time) such that

$$J(p) = \mathbb{E}\left[\exp(-r\tau_I^*)\left(\hat{J}_O(P(\tau_I^*)) - k_1P(\tau_I^*) - k_0\right)\Big|\, P(0)=p\right],$$

and an explicit expression of J.

Let us first consider a simple case. In this case, we have the following theorem.

Theorem 1.5.1 *Assume that* $k_1(r-\mu)+c_1 \geq 1$. *Then the optimal entry time* τ_I^* *is given by* $\tau_I^* = +\infty$ *a.s., i.e., the firm should never enter in the project. Furthermore the function* J *in* (1.5.1) *is given by* $J \equiv 0$.

Proof. (1) In this step, we will prove that if $k_1(r-\mu)+c_1 \geq 1$,

$$\mathbb{E}\left[\exp(-r\tau)\left(\hat{J}_O(P(\tau)) - k_1 P(\tau) - k_0\right)\Big| P(0)=p\right] \leq 0 \tag{1.5.2}$$

for any finite stopping time τ.

Define a function G by $G(p) := \hat{J}_O(p) - k_1 p - k_0$.

First, if one of the following conditions ① $l_1(r-\mu)-c_1 > -1$ and $c_0 \leq rl_0$, ② $l_1(r-\mu)-c_1 = -1$ and $c_0 < rl_0$ holds, the function $\hat{J}_O$ (see Theorem 1.4.2) is given by

$$\hat{J}_O(p) = \frac{1-c_1}{r-\mu}p - \frac{c_0}{r}.$$

Then we see that the inequality (1.5.2) holds if $k_1(r-\mu)+c_1 \geq 1$ since $G(p) \leq 0$.

Second, if $l_1(r-\mu)-c_1 \leq -1$ and $c_0 \geq rl_0$, the function $\hat{J}_O$ (see Theorem 1.4.3) is given by

$$\hat{J}_O(p) = -l_1 p - l_0.$$

Note that $l_1 + k_1 \geq 0$ and $l_0 + k_0 \geq 0$. It follows from $G(p) \leq 0$ that the inequality (1.5.2) holds in this case.

Third, if $l_1(r-\mu)-c_1 > -1$ and $c_0 > rl_0$, the function $\hat{J}_O$ is given by (see Theorem 1.4.5)

$$\hat{J}_O(p) = \begin{cases} A_1 p^{\lambda_1} + \dfrac{1-c_1}{r-\mu}p - \dfrac{c_0}{r}, & \text{if } p > p_O, \\ -l_1 p - l_0, & \text{if } p \leq p_O. \end{cases}$$

We have

$$G'(p) = \begin{cases} \lambda_1 A_1 p^{\lambda_1 - 1} + \dfrac{1-c_1-k_1(r-\mu)}{r-\mu}, & \text{if } p > p_O, \\ -l_1 - k_1, & \text{if } p \leq p_O, \end{cases}$$

from which we see that $G'(p) \leq 0$.

Note that $G(0) = -l_0 - k_0 \leq 0$. We have $G(p) \leq G(0) \leq 0$. Thus we find that the inequality (1.5.2) holds in this case.

Finally, Let us consider the case $l_1(r-\mu) - c_1 < -1$ and $c_0 < rl_0$. In this case, the function $\hat{J}_O$ is given by (see Theorem 1.4.7)

$$\hat{J}_O(p) = \begin{cases} A_1 p^{\lambda_2} + \dfrac{1-c_1}{r-\mu} p - \dfrac{c_0}{r}, & \text{if } p < p_O, \\ -l_1 p - l_0, & \text{if } p \geq p_O. \end{cases}$$

We have

$$G'(p) = \begin{cases} \lambda_2 A_1 p^{\lambda_2 - 1} + \dfrac{1 - c_1 - k_1(r-\mu)}{r-\mu}, & \text{if } p < p_O, \\ -l_1 - k_1, & \text{if } p \geq p_O, \end{cases}$$

from which we see that the function $G'(\cdot)$ is monotone increasing on $[0, +\infty)$.

It follows that $G'(p) \leq G'(p_O) = -l_1 - k_1 \leq 0$. Furthermore, we have

$$G(p) \leq G(0) = -\frac{c_0}{r} - k_0 \leq 0.$$

Thus we find that the inequality (1.5.2) holds in this case.

In summary, we have proved that if $k_1(r-\mu) + c_1 \geq 1$ the inequality (1.5.2) holds.

(2) Note that the function $G(\cdot)$ is a linear growth function by Lemma 1.4.4. It follows that there are two constants a_1 and a_0 such that

$$|\hat{J}_O(p) - k_1 p - k_0| \leq a_1 p + a_0.$$

Then, by some similar calculations to (1.4.7), we have

$$\lim_{T \to +\infty} \mathbb{E}\left[\exp(-rT)\left(\hat{J}_O(P(T)) - k_1 P(T) - k_0\right) \Big| P(0) = p\right] = 0.$$

Therefore, the optimal entry time τ_I^* is given by $\tau_I^* \equiv +\infty$ a.s. and the function J in (1.5.1) is given by $J \equiv 0$. □

Remark 1.5.2 If $l_1(r-\mu) - c_1 \leq -1$, the inequality $k_1(r-\mu) + c_1 \geq 1$ always holds since $k_1 + l_1 \geq 0$. Therefore, if $l_1(r-\mu) - c_1 \leq -1$, the firm should never enter the project.

Lemma 1.5.3 *The function $J(\cdot)$ is Lipschitz continuous on $[0,+\infty)$.*

Proof. The proof is similar to that of Lemma 1.4.4. □

Theorem 1.5.4 *Assume that $k_1(r-\mu)+c_1<1$, $l_1(r-\mu)-c_1>-1$ and $c_0 \le rl_0$. Then the function J in (1.5.1) is given by*

$$J(p)=\begin{cases} B_1 p^{\lambda_2}, & \text{if } 0<p<p_I,\\ \dfrac{1-c_1-k_1(r-\mu)}{r-\mu}p-\dfrac{c_0}{r}-k_0, & \text{if } p\ge p_I,\end{cases}$$

where

$$p_I=\frac{\lambda_2}{\lambda_2-1}\frac{r-\mu}{1-c_1-k_1(r-\mu)}\left(\frac{c_0}{r}+k_0\right),$$

and

$$B_1=\frac{1-c_1-k_1(r-\mu)}{r-\mu}p_I^{1-\lambda_2}-\left(\frac{c_0}{r}+k_0\right)p_I^{-\lambda_2}.$$

In addition, the optimal entry time τ_I^* is given by

$$\tau_I^*=\inf\{t: t>0 \text{ and } P(t)\ge p_I\}.$$

Before proving Theorem 1.5.4, we would like to explain the economic meaning of it. If $k_1(r-\mu)+c_1<1$, $l_1(r-\mu)-c_1>-1$ and $c_0\le rl_0$, the firm should not invest in the project when the commodity price is less than p_I in Theorem 1.5.4, and the maximal expected present value of the project is given by J in Theorem 1.5.4.

Proof of Theorem 1.5.4. (1) Recall the definition of the operator $\mathcal{L}$ [see (1.4.3)],

$$\mathcal{L}\zeta(t,p)=\frac{\partial\zeta}{\partial t}+\mu p\frac{\partial\zeta}{\partial p}+\frac{1}{2}\sigma^2p^2\frac{\partial^2\zeta}{\partial p^2}.$$

We make an *ansatz*

(1.5.3)

$$\psi(t,p)=\begin{cases}\exp(-rt)B_1p^{\lambda} \text{ in } D_I:=(0,+\infty)\times(0,p_I),\\ \exp(-rt)\left(\dfrac{1-c_1}{r-\mu}p-\dfrac{c_0}{r}-k_1p-k_0\right) \text{ on } (0,+\infty)\times[p_I,+\infty).\end{cases}$$

Then by (1.b) in the procedure for solving optimal stopping problems, we have

$$-r\exp(-rt)B_1p^{\lambda}+\mu\exp(-rt)pB_1\lambda p^{\lambda-1}+$$
$$\frac{1}{2}\sigma^2\exp(-rt)p^2B_1\lambda(\lambda-1)p^{\lambda-2}=0,$$

by which we require

$$-r+\mu\lambda+\frac{1}{2}\sigma^2\lambda(\lambda-1)=0.$$

Therefore, we have $\lambda=\lambda_1$ or $\lambda=\lambda_2$. Since the function J is Lipschitz continuous on $[0,+\infty)$ by Lemma 1.5.3, we must choose $\lambda=\lambda_2$.

By (1.a) in the procedure for solving optimal stopping problems, we have (1.5.4)

$$\begin{cases} B_1p_I^{\lambda_2}=\dfrac{1-c_1}{r-\mu}p_I-\dfrac{c_0}{r}-k_1p_I-k_0\left(=\dfrac{1-c_1-k_1(r-\mu)}{r-\mu}p_I-\dfrac{c_0}{r}-k_0\right) \\ \lambda_2B_1p_I^{\lambda_2-1}=\dfrac{1-c_1}{r-\mu}-k_1, \end{cases}$$

from which we obtain

$$p_I=\frac{\lambda_2}{\lambda_2-1}\times\frac{r-\mu}{1-c_1-k_1(r-\mu)}\left(\frac{c_0}{r}+k_0\right).$$

Furthermore,

$$\begin{aligned} B_1&=\left(\frac{1-c_1}{r-\mu}p_I-\frac{c_0}{r}-k_1p-k_0\right)p_I^{-\lambda_2} \\ &=\frac{1-c_1-k_1(r-\mu)}{r-\mu}p_I^{1-\lambda_2}-\left(\frac{c_0}{r}+k_0\right)p_I^{-\lambda_2}. \end{aligned}$$

We also have

$$B_1=\frac{1-c_1-k_1(r-\mu)}{r-\mu}p_I^{1-\lambda_2}\lambda_2^{-1}>0.$$

Now we have seen that the function (1.5.3) satisfies (1.a) and (1.b). We have to check (1.c) and (1.d).

(2) For (1.c) we only have to check that the inequality

$$\psi(t,p)>\exp(-rt)\left[\frac{1-c_1-k_1(r-\mu)}{r-\mu}p-\frac{c_0}{r}-k_0\right]$$

holds in D_I.

Define a function $h(p) := B_1 p^{\lambda_2} - \dfrac{1-c_1-k_1(r-\mu)}{r-\mu}p + \dfrac{c_0}{r} + k_0$. Then

$$h'(p) = \frac{1-c_1-k_1(r-\mu)}{r-\mu}\left[\left(\frac{p}{p_I}\right)^{\lambda_2-1} - 1\right] < 0$$

in $(0, p_I)$. Thus the function $h(p)$ is strictly monotone decreasing in $(0, p_I)$. On the other hand, we have $h(p_I) = 0$ by the construction of (1.5.3) (see the first equation of (1.5.4)). Thus $B_1 p^{\lambda_2} - \dfrac{1-c_1-k_1(r-\mu)}{r-\mu}p + \dfrac{c_0}{r} + k_0 > 0$ in $(0, p_I)$. So the inequality $\psi(t,p) > \exp(-rt)\left[\dfrac{1-c_1-k_1(r-\mu)}{r-\mu}p - \dfrac{c_0}{r} - k_0\right]$ holds in D_I.

(3) For (1.d) we only have to check that the inequality $\mathcal{L}\psi(t,p) \le 0$ holds in $(0,+\infty)\times(p_I,+\infty)$.

Since $\dfrac{1}{\lambda_2} > \dfrac{\mu}{r}$, $[1-c_1-k_1(r-\mu)]p_I = \dfrac{\lambda_2}{\lambda_2-1}(r-\mu)\left(\dfrac{c_0}{r}+k_0\right) > c_0 + rk_0$. Therefore, if $(t,p)\in(0,+\infty)\times(p_I,+\infty)$, we have

$$\mathcal{L}\psi(t,p) = -\exp(-rt)\left\{[1-c_1-k_1(r-\mu)]p - c_0 - rk_0\right\} < 0.$$

(4) Note that

$$\frac{\partial^2\psi}{\partial p^2}(0,p) = \begin{cases} \lambda_2(\lambda_2-1)B_1 p^{\lambda_2-2}, & \text{if } 0<p<p_I, \\ 0, & \text{if } p > p_I. \end{cases}$$

We can repeat Step 4 of the proof of Theorem 1.4.5. Then for any stopping time τ, we have

(1.5.5)
$$\mathbb{E}\left[\exp(-r\tau)\left(\frac{1-c_1-k_1(r-\mu)}{r-\mu}P(\tau) - \frac{c_0}{r} - k_0\right)\middle| P(0)=p\right] \le \psi(0,p).$$

(5) Take $\tau = \tau_I^*$ in the definition of τ_k (see Step 4 of the proof of Theorem

1.4.5). Then

$$\begin{aligned}
&\mathbb{E}\left[\psi(\tau_k, P(\tau_k))\middle| P(0)=p\right] \\
&= \mathbb{E}\left[\psi(\tau_k, P(\tau_k))\mathbf{1}_{\{\tau_I^* \le k\wedge S_k\}}\middle| P(0)=p\right] + \\
&\quad \mathbb{E}\left[\psi(\tau_k, P(\tau_k))\mathbf{1}_{\{\tau_I^* > k\wedge S_k\}}\middle| P(0)=p\right] \\
&= \mathbb{E}\Bigg[\exp(-r\tau_I^*)\Bigg(\frac{1-c_1-k_1(r-\mu)}{r-\mu}P(\tau_I^*) - \\
&\quad \frac{c_0}{r} - k_0\Bigg)\mathbf{1}_{\{\tau_I^* \le k\wedge S_k\}}\Bigg| P(0)=p\Bigg] + \\
&\quad \mathbb{E}\left[\psi(\tau_k, P(\tau_k))\mathbf{1}_{\{\tau_I^* > k\wedge S_k\}}\middle| P(0)=p\right].
\end{aligned} \tag{1.5.6}$$

We need to estimate $\mathbb{E}\left[\psi(\tau_k, P(\tau_k))\mathbf{1}_{\{\tau_I^* > k\wedge S_k\}}\middle| P(0)=p\right]$ (the last term of (1.5.6)).

$$\begin{aligned}
&\mathbb{E}\left[\exp\left(-r(k\wedge S_k)\right) P(k\wedge S_k)^{\lambda_2}\mathbf{1}_{\{\tau_I^* > k\wedge S_k\}}\middle| P(0)=p\right] \\
&\le p_I^{\lambda_2}\mathbb{E}\left[\exp\left(-r(k\wedge S_k)\right)\mathbf{1}_{\{\tau_I^* > k\wedge S_k\}}\middle| P(0)=p\right] \\
&\le p_I^{\lambda_2}\mathbb{E}\left[\exp\left(-r(k\wedge S_k)\right)\middle| P(0)=p\right].
\end{aligned}$$

Thus

$$\lim_{k\to+\infty}\mathbb{E}\left[\psi(\tau_k, P(\tau_k))\mathbf{1}_{\{\tau_I^* > k\wedge S_k\}}\middle| P(0)=p\right] = 0.$$

Now by a similar method to that in Step 5 of the proof of Theorem 1.4.5, we have

$$\mathbb{E}\left[\exp(-r\tau_I^*)\left(\frac{1-c_1-k_1(r-\mu)}{r-\mu}P(\tau_I^*) - \frac{c_0}{r} - k_0\right)\middle| P(0)=p\right] = \psi(0,p). \tag{1.5.7}$$

Combining (1.5.5) and (1.5.7), we have proved that $J(p)=\psi(0,p)$ and $\tau_I^* = \inf\{t : t>0 \text{ and } P(t)\ge p_I\}$. □

Corollary 1.5.5 *The optimal entry trigger price p_I in Theorem 1.5.4 satisfies* $p_I > \dfrac{c_0 + rk_0}{1-c_1-k_1(r-\mu)}$.

Proof. See Step 3 of the proof of Theorem 1.5.4. □

Before stating the following lemma, let us first recall some parameters defined in Step 1 of the proof of Theorem 1.4.5. That is,

$$\begin{aligned} p_O &= \frac{\lambda_1}{\lambda_1-1}\times\frac{r-\mu}{1-c_1+l_1(r-\mu)}\left(\frac{c_0}{r}-l_0\right), \\ A_1 &= \frac{1-c_1+l_1(r-\mu)}{\lambda_1(\mu-r)}{p_O}^{1-\lambda_1}, \\ A_2 &= \frac{1-c_1}{r-\mu}, \text{ and} \\ A_3 &= -\frac{c_0}{r}. \end{aligned}$$

Lemma 1.5.6 *Assume that* $k_1(r-\mu)+c_1<1$, $l_1(r-\mu)-c_1>-1$ *and* $c_0>rl_0$. *Define a function* E *by*

$$E(p) := A_1(\lambda_2-\lambda_1)p^{\lambda_1}+(A_2-k_1)(\lambda_2-1)p+\lambda_2(A_3-k_0).$$

Then the equation $E(p)=0$ *has only two solutions* p_1 *and* p_2 *in* $(0,+\infty)$ *satisfying* $p_1\le p_O$ *and* $p_2>p_O$. *In addition, the solution* p_2 *satisfies* $\lambda_1A_1p_2^{\lambda_1-1}+A_2-k_1>0$.

Proof. (1) Suppose that the equation $E(p)=0$ has three solutions in $(0,+\infty)$. Then by Rolle's mean value theorem, there is a positive number ξ such that $E''(\xi)=0$, i.e.,

$$A_1(\lambda_2-\lambda_1)\lambda_1(\lambda_1-1)\xi^{\lambda_1-2}=0,$$

which is impossible. Thus the equation $E(p)=0$ has at most two solutions in $(0,+\infty)$.

(2) In this step, we will estimate $E(p_O)$ and $E'(p_O)$.

We first estimate $E(p_O)$ as follows.

$$\begin{aligned} E(p_O) &= \left[\frac{\lambda_2-\lambda_1}{1-\lambda_1}+\frac{1-c_1-k_1(r-\mu)}{1-c_1+l_1(r-\mu)}\times\frac{\lambda_1(\lambda_2-1)}{\lambda_1-1}\right]\left(\frac{c_0}{r}-l_0\right)- \\ &\quad \lambda_2\left(\frac{c_0}{r}+k_0\right) \\ &\le \left[\frac{\lambda_2-\lambda_1}{1-\lambda_1}+\frac{\lambda_1(\lambda_2-1)}{\lambda_1-1}\right]\left(\frac{c_0}{r}-l_0\right)-\lambda_2\left(\frac{c_0}{r}+k_0\right) \\ &= -\lambda_2(k_0+l_0)\le 0, \end{aligned}$$

where we have used $k_1 + l_1 \geq 0$ for the first inequality and $k_0 + l_0 \geq 0$ for the second inequality.

Now we estimate $E'(p_O)$.

$$\begin{aligned} E'(p_O) &= \frac{1-c_1}{r-\mu}(\lambda_1 - 1) - l_1(\lambda_2 - \lambda_1) - k_1(\lambda_2 - 1) \\ &\leq \frac{1-c_1}{r-\mu}(\lambda_1 - 1) - k_1(\lambda_1 - 1) \\ &= \frac{1 - c_1 - k_1(r-\mu)}{r-\mu}(\lambda_1 - 1) < 0, \end{aligned}$$

where we have used $k_1 + l_1 \geq 0$ for the first inequality.

(3) Note that $\lim\limits_{p\to 0+} E(p) = +\infty$, $\lim\limits_{p\to+\infty} E(p) = +\infty$, $E(p_O) \leq 0$ and $E'(p_O) < 0$. We find that the equation $E(p) = 0$ has only two solutions p_1 and p_2 in $(0, +\infty)$ satisfying $p_1 \leq p_O$ and $p_2 > p_O$.

Furthermore, $E'(p_2) > 0$. It follows that

$$\begin{aligned} \lambda_1 A_1 p_2^{\lambda_1 - 1} + A_2 - k_1 &> \lambda_1 A_1 p_2^{\lambda_1 - 1} + \frac{\lambda_2 - 1}{\lambda_2 - \lambda_1}(A_2 - k_1) \\ &= \frac{1}{\lambda_2 - \lambda_1} E'(p_2) > 0. \end{aligned}$$

The proof is complete. □

Theorem 1.5.7 *Assume that* $k_1(r-\mu) - c_1 < 1$, $l_1(r-\mu) - c_1 > -1$ *and* $c_0 > rl_0$. *Then the function* J *in* (1.5.1) *is given by*

$$J(p) = \begin{cases} B_1 p^{\lambda_2}, & \text{if } 0 < p < p_I, \\ \hat{J}_O(p) - k_1 p - k_0, & \text{if } p \geq p_I, \end{cases}$$

where $p_I = p_2$ *and* $B_1 = \dfrac{(1-\lambda_1)[1 - c_1 - k_1(r-\mu)]}{(r-\mu)(\lambda_2 - \lambda_1)} p_I^{1-\lambda_2} + \dfrac{\lambda_1}{\lambda_2 - \lambda_1}\Big(\dfrac{c_0}{r} + k_0\Big) p_I^{-\lambda_2}$. *For the definition of* $\hat{J}_O$, *see Theorem 1.4.5.*

In addition, the optimal entry time τ_I^* *is given by*

$$\tau_I^* = \inf\{t : t > 0 \text{ and } P(t) \geq p_I\}.$$

Proof. (1) Recall the definition of the operator $\mathcal{L}$ [see (1.4.3)],

$$\mathcal{L}\zeta(t,p) = \frac{\partial \zeta}{\partial t} + \mu p \frac{\partial \zeta}{\partial p} + \frac{1}{2}\sigma^2 p^2 \frac{\partial^2 \zeta}{\partial p^2}.$$

We make an *ansatz*

$$
\psi(t,p) = \begin{cases} \exp(-rt)B_1 p^{\lambda} \text{ in } D_I := (0,+\infty)\times(0,p_I), \\ \exp(-rt)\left(\hat{J}_O(p) - k_1 p - k_0\right) \text{ on } (0,+\infty)\times[p_I,+\infty). \end{cases} \tag{1.5.8}
$$

Then by (1.b) in the procedure for solving optimal stopping problems, we have

$$
\begin{aligned}
&-r\exp(-rt)B_1p^{\lambda} + \mu\exp(-rt)pB_1\lambda p^{\lambda-1} + \\
&\frac{1}{2}\sigma^2\exp(-rt)p^2B_1\lambda(\lambda-1)p^{\lambda-2} = 0,
\end{aligned}
$$

from which we obtain

$$
-r + \mu\lambda + \frac{1}{2}\sigma^2\lambda(\lambda-1) = 0.
$$

Therefore, we have $\lambda = \lambda_1$ or $\lambda = \lambda_2$. Since the function $J(\cdot)$ is Lipschitz continuous on $[0,+\infty)$ by Lemma 1.5.3, we must choose $\lambda = \lambda_2$.

By (1.a) in the procedure for solving optimal stopping problems, we have

$$
\begin{cases} B_1 p_I^{\lambda_2} = \hat{J}_O(p_I) - k_1 p_I - k_0 \\ \lambda_2 B_1 p_I^{\lambda_2 - 1} = \hat{J}'_O(p_I) - k_1. \end{cases} \tag{1.5.9}
$$

Let us require $p_I > p_O$, because with this requirement we can prove that the function ψ satisfies all the properties in the the procedure for solving optimal stopping problems. Therefore, we have

$$
A_1(\lambda_2 - \lambda_1)p_I^{\lambda_1} + (A_2 - k_1)(\lambda_2 - 1)p_I + \lambda_2(A_3 - k_0) = 0. \tag{1.5.10}
$$

It follows that $p_I = p_1$ or $p_I = p_2$ by Lemma 1.5.6. Thus we must choose $p_I = p_2$. Furthermore,

$$
\begin{aligned}
B_1 &= \left(\hat{J}_O(p_I) - k_1 p_I - k_0\right) p_I^{-\lambda_2} \\
&= \frac{(1-\lambda_1)[1 - c_1 - k_1(r-\mu)]}{(r-\mu)(\lambda_2 - \lambda_1)} p_I^{1-\lambda_2} + \frac{\lambda_1}{\lambda_2 - \lambda_1}\left(\frac{c_0}{r} + k_0\right) p_I^{-\lambda_2},
\end{aligned}
$$

where we have used the first equation of (1.5.9) for the first equality and (1.5.10) for the second equality. We also have $B_1 = (\hat{J}'_O(p_I) - k_1)p_I^{1-\lambda_2}\lambda_2^{-1} > 0$ by Lemma 1.5.6.

Now we have seen that the function (1.5.8) satisfies (1.a) and (1.b). We have to check (1.c) and (1.d).

(2) For (1.c) we only have to check that the inequality

$$\psi(t,p) > \exp(-rt)\left(\hat{J}_O(p) - k_1 p - k_0\right)$$

holds in D_I. We need to prove that the inequality $B_1 p^{\lambda_2} > \hat{J}_O(p) - k_1 p - k_0$ holds if $0 < p < p_I$.

First, we prove that the inequality $B_1 p^{\lambda_2} > \hat{J}_O(p) - k_1 p - k_0$ holds if $0 < p \leq p_O$.

Note that $B_1 > 0$ by Step 1. Then

$$B_1 p^{\lambda_2} - \hat{J}_O(p) + k_1 p + k_0 = B_1 p^{\lambda_2} + l_1 p + l_0 + k_1 p + k_0 > 0 \text{ on } (0, p_O].$$

Therefore, we see that the inequality $B_1 p^{\lambda_2} > \hat{J}_O(p) - k_1 p - k_0$ holds if $0 < p \leq p_O$.

Second, we prove that the inequality $B_1 p^{\lambda_2} > \hat{J}_O(p) - k_1 p - k_0$ holds if $p_O < p < p_I$.

Define a function $U(p) := B_1 p^{\lambda_2} - \left(\hat{J}_O(p) - k_1 p - k_0\right) = B_1 p^{\lambda_2} - A_1 p^{\lambda_1} - (A_2 - k_1)p - A_3 + k_0$ on $[p_O, p_I]$. Since $B_1 > 0$ and $\hat{J}_O(p_O) = -l_1 p_O - l_0$, we have $U(p_O) = B_1 p_O^{\lambda_2} + (k_1 + l_1)p_O + k_0 + l_0 > 0$. We also have $U(p_I) = 0$ by the construction of the function ψ (see the first equation of (1.5.9)).

Furthermore, $U'(p) = B_1\lambda_2 p^{\lambda_2 - 1} - A_1\lambda_1 p^{\lambda_1 - 1} - A_2 + k_1$ and $U''(p) = B_1\lambda_2(\lambda_2 - 1)p^{\lambda_2 - 2} - A_1\lambda_1(\lambda_1 - 1)p^{\lambda_1 - 2}$. Thus the equation $U''(p) = 0$ has at most one solution in (p_O, p_I).

If the equation $U''(p) = 0$ has no solution in (p_O, p_I), then $U'(\cdot)$ is a strictly monotonic function on $[p_O, p_I]$. Since $B_1 > 0$, we have $U'(p_O) = \lambda_2 B_1 p_O^{\lambda_2 - 1} + k_1 + l_1 > 0$, where we have used the second equation of (1.4.9). Note that $U'(p_I) = 0$ by the construction of the function ψ (see the second equation of (1.5.9)). Then we get $U'(p) > 0$ if $p_O < p < p_I$. Consequently $0 < U(p_O) < U(p_I) = 0$, which is a contradiction.

Up to now we have shown that the equation $U''(p) = 0$ has only one solution ξ in (p_O, p_I). So there are only the following two cases: ① $U''(p) > 0$ in (p_O, ξ) and $U''(p) < 0$ in (ξ, p_I); ② $U''(p) < 0$ in (p_O, ξ) and $U''(p) > 0$ in (ξ, p_I).

If $U''(p) > 0$ in (p_O, ξ) and $U''(p) < 0$ in (ξ, p_I), then the function $U'(\cdot)$ is strictly monotone increasing on $[p_O, \xi]$ and strictly monotone decreasing on $[\xi, p_I]$. Noting that $U'(p_O) > 0$ and $U'(p_I) = 0$, we find that $U'(p) > 0$ if $p_O < p < p_I$. Therefore, $0 < U(p_O) < U(p_I) = 0$, which is a contradiction.

Let us summarize the discussion we just give. In fact we have proved the following claim.

`Claim` The equation $U''(p) = 0$ has only one solution ξ in (p_O, p_I) satisfying that $U''(p) < 0$ in (p_O, ξ) and that $U''(p) > 0$ in (ξ, p_I).

Note that $U'(p_O) > 0$ and $U'(p_I) = 0$. Then by the above claim we see that there is a real number θ such that $U'(p) > 0$ in (p_O, θ) and $U'(p) < 0$ in (θ, p_I). Therefore, $U(p) > U(p_O) > 0$ in (p_O, θ) and $U(p) > U(p_I) = 0$ on $[\theta, p_I)$. Now we have proved that the inequality $B_1 p^{\lambda_2} > \hat{J}_O(p) - k_1 p - k_0$ holds if $p_O < p < p_I$.

(3) For (1.d) we only have to check that the inequality $\mathcal{L}\psi(t,p) \leq 0$ holds in $(0, +\infty) \times (p_I, +\infty)$.

Note that $U''(p) > 0$ if $\xi < p < p_I$ by the claim in Step 2. Then

$$\frac{\partial^2 \psi}{\partial p^2}(t, {p_I}^+) < \frac{\partial^2 \psi}{\partial p^2}(t, {p_I}^-).$$

It follows that

$$\begin{aligned} &-\exp(-rt)\{[1 - c_1 - k_1(r-\mu)]p_I - c_0 - rk_0\} \\ &= \mathcal{L}\psi(t, {p_I}^+) < \mathcal{L}\psi(t, {p_I}^-) = 0. \end{aligned} \tag{1.5.11}$$

Therefore, if $(t,p) \in (0, +\infty) \times (p_I, +\infty)$, we have

$$\mathcal{L}\psi(t,p) = -\exp(-rt)\,\{[1 - c_1 - k_1(r-\mu)]p - c_0 - rk_0\} < 0.$$

(4) Note that

$$\frac{\partial^2 \psi}{\partial p^2}(0,p) = \begin{cases} \lambda_2(\lambda_2 - 1)B_1 p^{\lambda_2 - 2}, & \text{if } 0 < p < p_I, \\ \lambda_1(\lambda_1 - 1)A_1 p^{\lambda_1 - 2}, & \text{if } p > p_I. \end{cases}$$

We can repeat Step 4 of the proof of Theorem 1.4.5. Then for any stopping time τ, we have

$$\mathbb{E}\left[\exp(-r\tau)\left(\hat{J}_O(P(\tau)) - k_1 P(\tau) - k_0\right)\Big|\, P(0) = p\right] \leq \psi(0,p). \tag{1.5.12}$$

(5) Take $\tau = \tau_I^*$ in the definition of τ_k (see Step 4 of the proof of Theorem 1.4.5). Then we repeat Step 5 of the proof of Theorem 1.5.4 and find that

$$(1.5.13)\quad \mathbb{E}\left[\exp(-r\tau_I^*)\left(\hat{J}_O(P(\tau_I^*)) - k_1 P(\tau_I^*) - k_0\right)\middle| P(0) = p\right] = \psi(0, p).$$

Combining (1.5.12) and (1.5.13), we have proved that $J(p) = \psi(0, p)$ and $\tau_I^* = \inf\{t : t > 0 \text{ and } P(t) \geq p_I\}$. □

Remark 1.5.8 The statement in Step 2 of the proof of Theorem 1.5.7, i.e.,

the inequality $B_1 p^{\lambda_2} > \hat{J}_O(p) - k_1 p - k_0$ holds if $0 < p < p_I$,

can be proved visually by geometry. See Figure 1.1.

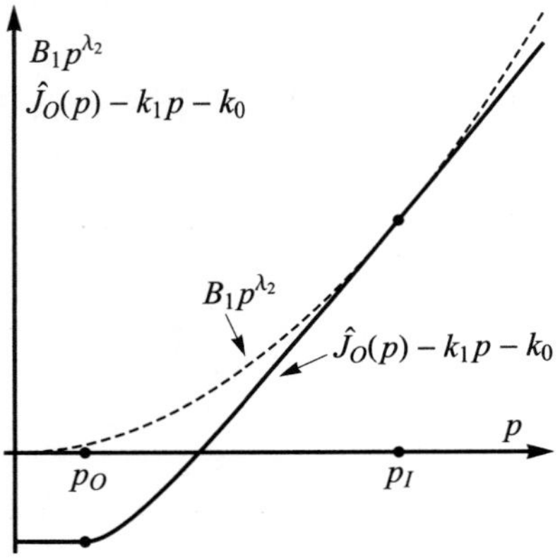

Figure 1.1 $B_1 p^{\lambda_2} > \hat{J}_O(p) - k_1 p - k_0$ if $0 < p < p_I$

Corollary 1.5.9 *The optimal entry trigger price p_I in Theorem 1.5.7 satisfies* $p_I > \dfrac{c_0 + r k_0}{1 - c_1 - k_1(r - \mu)}$.

Proof. See Step 3 of the proof of Theorem 1.5.7. In particular, see (1.5.11). □

Now we state the main result in this chapter.

Theorem 1.5.10 *Assume that the price process P satisfies*

$$\mathrm{d}P(t) = \mu P(t)\mathrm{d}t + \sigma P(t)\mathrm{d}B(t), \text{ and } P(0) > 0,$$

where $\mu \in \mathbb{R}$, $\sigma > 0$, and B is a one dimensional standard Brownian motion, and that the running cost C, the initial investment cost K_I and the terminal investment cost K_O are taken the following forms:

$$C(p) = c_1 p + c_0,$$
$$K_I(p) = k_1 p + k_0,$$
$$K_O(p) = l_1 p + l_0,$$

respectively. Here, c_i, k_i and l_i are some constants, $i = 0, 1$, such that $c_0 \geq 0$, $k_0 \geq 0$, $k_0 + l_0 \geq 0$ and $k_1 + l_1 \geq 0$. Furthermore, assume that the discount rate r is positive such that $r > \mu$. Let λ_1 and λ_2 be the two solutions which satisfy $\lambda_1 < 0$ and $\lambda_2 > 1$ of the quadratic equation

$$-r + \mu\lambda + \frac{1}{2}\sigma^2\lambda(\lambda - 1) = 0.$$

Consider the optimal problem

(1.5.14)

$$\hat{J}_{IO}(p) := \sup_{0 \leq \tau_I \leq \tau_O} \mathbb{E}\bigg[\int_{\tau_I}^{\tau_O} \exp(-rt)(P(t) - c_1 P(t) - c_0)\mathrm{d}t -$$
$$\exp(-r\tau_I)\left(k_1 P(\tau_I) + k_0\right) - \exp(-r\tau_O)\left(l_1 P(\tau_O) + l_0\right) \big| \, P(0) = p\bigg].$$

Then

① *If $k_1(r-\mu)+c_1 \geq 1$, then the optimal entry time τ_I^* is given by $\tau_I^* = +\infty$ a.s. and the function $\hat{J}_{IO}$ in* (1.5.14) *is given by $\hat{J}_{IO} \equiv 0$.*

② *If $k_1(r-\mu)+c_1 < 1$, $l_1(r-\mu)-c_1 > -1$ and $c_0 \leq rl_0$, then the optimal entry time τ_I^* is given by $\tau_I^* = \inf\{t : t > 0$ and $P(t) \geq p_I\}$, the optimal exit time τ_O^* is given by $\tau_O^* = +\infty$ a.s. and the function $\hat{J}_{IO}$ in* (1.5.14) *is given by*

$$\hat{J}_{IO}(p) = \begin{cases} B_1 p^{\lambda_2}, & \text{if } 0 < p < p_I, \\ \dfrac{1 - c_1 - k_1(r-\mu)}{r-\mu}p - \dfrac{c_0}{r} - k_0, & \text{if } p \geq p_I, \end{cases}$$

where $p_I = \dfrac{\lambda_2}{\lambda_2 - 1}\dfrac{r-\mu}{1 - c_1 - k_1(r-\mu)}\left(\dfrac{c_0}{r} + k_0\right)$, and $B_1 = \dfrac{1 - c_1 - k_1(r-\mu)}{r-\mu} \times$ $p_I^{1-\lambda_2} - \left(\dfrac{c_0}{r} + k_0\right)p_I^{-\lambda_2}$.

③ *If* $k_1(r-\mu)+c_1<1$, $l_1(r-\mu)-c_1>-1$ *and* $c_0>rl_0$, *then the optimal entry time* τ_I^* *is given by* $\tau_I^*=\inf\{t:t>0$ *and* $P(t)\geq p_I\}$, *the optimal exit time* τ_O^* *is given by* $\tau_O^*=\inf\{t:t>\tau_I^*$ *and* $P(t)\leq p_O\}$ *and the function* $\hat{J}_{IO}$ *in* (1.5.14) *is given by*

$$\hat{J}_{IO}(p)=\begin{cases}B_1p^{\lambda_2}, & \text{if } 0<p<p_I,\\ A_1p^{\lambda_1}+\dfrac{1-c_1-k_1(r-\mu)}{r-\mu}p-\dfrac{c_0}{r}-k_0, & \text{if } p\geq p_I,\end{cases}$$

where $p_O=\dfrac{\lambda_1}{\lambda_1-1}\times\dfrac{r-\mu}{1-c_1+l_1(r-\mu)}\left(\dfrac{c_0}{r}-l_0\right)$, $A_1=\dfrac{1-c_1+l_1(r-\mu)}{\lambda_1(\mu-r)}\times$ $p_O^{1-\lambda_1}$, p_I *is the largest solution of the following equation*

$$A_1(\lambda_2-\lambda_1)p^{\lambda_1}+\frac{1-c_1-k_1(r-\mu)}{r-\mu}(\lambda_2-1)p-\lambda_2\left(\frac{c_0}{r}+k_0\right)=0,$$

and $B_1=\dfrac{(1-\lambda_1)[1-c_1-k_1(r-\mu)]}{(r-\mu)(\lambda_2-\lambda_1)}p_I^{1-\lambda_2}+\left(\dfrac{c_0}{r}+k_0\right)\dfrac{\lambda_1}{\lambda_2-\lambda_1}p_I^{-\lambda_2}$.

Remark 1.5.11 If $l_1(r-\mu)-c_1\leq-1$, then $k_1(r-\mu)+c_1\geq1$ because $k_1+l_1\geq0$.

Proof of Theorem 1.5.10. (1) Recall the definition of the function J [see (1.5.1)],

$$J(p):=\sup_{0\leq\tau_I}\mathbb{E}\left[\exp(-r\tau_I)\left(\hat{J}_O(P(\tau_I))-k_1P(\tau_I)-k_0\right)\Big|\,P(0)=p\right].$$

We will prove that $J(p)=\hat{J}_{IO}(p)$ for $p\in[0,+\infty)$.

(2) Define a sequence of stopping times $(R_k,k\in\mathbb{N})$ by $R_k:=\inf\{t:t>0,P(t)>k\}$. For an entry time τ_I, define a sequence of stopping times $(S_k,k\in\mathbb{N})$ by $S_k:=\tau_I\wedge k\wedge R_k$. Similarly, for an exit time $\tau_O(\geq\tau_I)$, define a sequence of stopping times $(T_k,k\in\mathbb{N})$ by $T_k:=\tau_O\wedge k\wedge R_k$. Define an operator $\mathcal{A}$ by

$$\mathcal{A}\varphi(p):=\frac{1}{2}\sigma^2p^2\varphi''(p)+\mu p\varphi'(p)-r\varphi(p).$$

Note that the functions $\hat{J}_O$ and J are C^1 convex functions. It follows from Meyer-Itô formula (see [38, p. 218, Theorem 70]) that

$$\exp(-rT_k)\hat{J}_O(P(T_k))=\exp(-rS_k)\hat{J}_O(P(S_k))+\int_{S_k}^{T_k}\exp(-rt)\mathcal{A}\hat{J}_O(P(t))\mathrm{d}t+$$
$$\sigma\int_{S_k}^{T_k}\exp(-rt)P(t)\hat{J}_O'(P(t))\mathrm{d}B(t),$$

$$\exp(-rS_k)J(P(S_k)) = J(P(0)) + \int_0^{S_k} \exp(-rt)\mathcal{A}J(P(t))\mathrm{d}t + \sigma \int_0^{S_k} \exp(-rt)P(t)J'(P(t))\mathrm{d}B(t).$$

Therefore,

(1.5.15)

$$\begin{aligned}
&\int_{S_k}^{T_k} \exp(-rt)\left(P(t) - c_1P(t) - c_0\right)\mathrm{d}t - \exp(-rS_k)(k_1P(S_k) + k_0) - \\
&\exp(-rT_k)(l_1P(T_k) + l_0) \\
=&\int_{S_k}^{T_k} \exp(-rt)\left(\mathcal{A}\hat{J}_O(P(t)) + P(t) - c_1P(t) - c_0\right)\mathrm{d}t + \\
&\int_0^{S_k} \exp(-rt)\mathcal{A}J(P(t))\mathrm{d}t - \\
&\exp(-rS_k)(k_1P(S_k) + k_0 - \hat{J}_O(P(S_k)) + J(P(S_k))) - \\
&\exp(-rT_k)(l_1P(T_k) + l_0 + \hat{J}_O(P(T_k))) + \\
&\sigma\int_{S_k}^{T_k} \exp(-rt)P(t)\hat{J}'_O(P(t))\mathrm{d}B(t) + \\
&\sigma\int_0^{S_k} \exp(-rt)P(t)J'(P(t))\mathrm{d}B(t) + J(P(0)).
\end{aligned}$$

(3) By the optimal stopping theorem (see [29, p. 175, Theorem 7.12]), we have

$$\mathbb{E}\left[\int_{S_k}^{T_k} \exp(-rt)P(t)\hat{J}'_O(P(t))\mathrm{d}B(t)\middle| P(0) = p\right] = 0,$$

$$\mathbb{E}\left[\int_0^{S_k} \exp(-rt)P(t)J'(P(t))\mathrm{d}B(t)\middle| P(0) = p\right] = 0.$$

In addition, note that

$$\mathcal{A}\hat{J}_O(p) + p - c_1p - c_0 \leq 0,$$

$$l_1p + l_0 + \hat{J}_O(p) \geq 0,$$

$$\mathcal{A}J(p) \leq 0,$$

$$k_1p + k_0 - \hat{J}_O(p) + J(p) \geq 0.$$

Then it follows from (1.5.15) that

$$\mathbb{E}\bigg[\int_{S_k}^{T_k} \exp(-rt)\,(P(t) - c_1 P(t) - c_0)\,\mathrm{d}t - \exp(-rS_k)(k_1 P(S_k) + k_0) -$$
$$\exp(-rT_k)(l_1 P(T_k) + l_0)|\, P(0) = p\bigg] \le J(p).$$

Taking limits in the above inequality and using Lemma 1.4.1 and (1.4.7), we get

(1.5.16)
$$\mathbb{E}\bigg[\int_{\tau_I}^{\tau_O} \exp(-rt)\,(P(t) - c_1 P(t) - c_0)\,\mathrm{d}t - \exp(-r\tau_I)(k_1 P(\tau_I) + k_0) -$$
$$\exp(-r\tau_O)(l_1 P(\tau_O) + l_0)|\, P(0) = p\bigg] \le J(p).$$

Thus

$$\hat{J}_{IO}(p) \le J(p). \tag{1.5.17}$$

(4) The conclusion ① follows from Theorem 1.5.1 and (1.5.17).

(5) Assume that $k_1(r-\mu)+c_1 < 1$, $l_1(r-\mu)-c_1 > -1$ and $c_0 \le rl_0$. Take $\tau_I = \tau_I^*$ in the definition of S_k and $\tau_O = \tau_O^*$ in the definition of T_k, where τ_I^* and τ_O^* are given by $\tau_I^* = \inf\{t : t > 0$ and $P(t) \ge p_I\}$ and $\tau_O^* = +\infty$ a.s., respectively.

Note that

$$\mathcal{A}J(P(t)) = 0 \text{ for } 0 < t < \tau_I^* \text{ by Theorem 1.5.4,}$$

and

$$\mathcal{A}\hat{J}_O(P(t)) + P(t) - c_1 P(t) - c_0 = 0 \text{ for } \tau_I^* < t < \tau_O^* \text{ by Theorem 1.4.2.}$$

Then, from (1.5.15), we have

$$\mathbb{E}\bigg[\int_{S_k}^{T_k} \exp(-rt)\,(P(t) - c_1 P(t) - c_0)\,\mathrm{d}t - \exp(-rS_k)(k_1 P(S_k) + k_0) -$$
$$\exp(-rT_k)(l_1 P(T_k) + l_0)|\, P(0) = p\bigg]$$
$$= -\,\mathbb{E}\Big[\exp(-rS_k)(k_1 P(S_k) + k_0 - \hat{J}_O(P(S_k)) + J(P(S_k))) +$$
$$\exp(-rT_k)(l_1 P(T_k) + l_0 + \hat{J}_O(P(T_k)))\Big|\, P(0) = p\Big] + J(p).$$

See Theorem 1.5.4 for the definition of the function J.

Since the functions J and $\hat{J}_O$ are at most linear growth, we find, by a similar way to that of (1.5.16),

$$\mathbb{E}\Bigg[\int_{\tau_I^*}^{\tau_O^*} \exp(-rt)\,(P(t) - c_1 P(t) - c_0)\,\mathrm{d}t - \exp(-r\tau_I^*)(k_1 P(\tau_I^*) + k_0) - \exp(-r\tau_O^*)(l_1 P(\tau_O^*) + l_0) \Big|\, P(0) = p\Bigg] = J(p).$$

Similarly, the conclusion ③ holds, but using Theorem 1.4.5 and Theorem 1.5.7. □

We give here a numerical example to demonstrate how to use Theorem 1.5.10.

The related parameters are assigned as follows: $c_1 = 0.2$, $c_0 = 10$, $k_1 = 0.2$, $k_0 = 30$, $l_1 = -0.2$, $l_0 = -5$, $r = 0.05$, $\mu = 0.03$ and $\sigma = 0.2$. We adopt the following procedure.

Step 1 Since $k_1(r-\mu) + c_1 = 0.204 < 1$, $l_1(r-\mu) - c_1 = -0.204 > -1$ and $c_0 = 10 > -0.05 \times 5 = rl_0$, we need to apply the conclusion ③ in Theorem 1.5.10.

Step 2 The equation

$$-r + \mu\lambda + \frac{1}{2}\sigma^2\lambda(\lambda - 1) = 0$$

is interpreted as

$$-0.05 + 0.03\lambda + 0.02\lambda(\lambda - 1) = 0.$$

By solving the above equation, we have $\lambda_1 = -1.85078$ and $\lambda_2 = 1.35078$. Furthermore,

$$p_O = \frac{\lambda_1}{\lambda_1 - 1} \times \frac{r - \mu}{1 - c_1 + l_1(r - \mu)}\left(\frac{c_0}{r} - l_0\right) = 3.34397$$

and $A_1 = \dfrac{1 - c_1 + l_1(r-\mu)}{\lambda_1(\mu - r)}{p_O}^{1-\lambda_1} = 671.559.$

Step 3 The equation

$$A_1(\lambda_2 - \lambda_1)p^{\lambda_1} + \frac{1 - c_1 - k_1(r-\mu)}{r - \mu}(\lambda_2 - 1)p - \lambda_2\left(\frac{c_0}{r} + k_0\right) = 0$$

is read as

$$2150.04p^{-1.85078} + 13.9611p - 310.679 = 0.$$

The largest solution of the above equation is 21.7372.

Thus $p_I = 21.7372$ and

$$B_1 = \frac{(1-\lambda_1)[1-c_1-k_1(r-\mu)]}{(r-\mu)(\lambda_2-\lambda_1)} p_I^{1-\lambda_2} + \frac{\lambda_1}{\lambda_2-\lambda_1}\left(\frac{c_O}{r}+k_O\right) p_I^{-\lambda_2} = 9.95718.$$

Step 4 The optimal entry time τ_I^* is given by $\tau_I^* = \inf\{t : t > 0 \text{ and } P(t) \geq 21.7372\}$, the optimal exit time τ_O^* is given by $\tau_O^* = \inf\{t : t > \tau_I^* \text{ and } P(t) \leq 3.34397\}$ and the maximal expected present value $\hat{J}_{IO}$ of the project is given by

$$\hat{J}_{IO}(p) = \begin{cases} 9.95718p^{1.35078}, & \text{if } 0 < p < 21.7372, \\ 671.559p^{-1.85078} + 39.8p - 230, & \text{if } p \geq 21.7372. \end{cases}$$

1.6 Conclusions

In the real world, some investment costs of a project may depend on the price of the commodity produced by the project. For instance, as the commodity price increases, workers would claim for a higher salary. Therefore, it is reasonable to decompose every cost into two parts. One part is fixed, and the other part is related to the commodity price. In the present chapter, we have taken a simple decomposition by assuming that the costs are linear functions of the commodity price. Under this assumption, from the standpoint of stochastic programming, we rigorously analyse entry-exit decisions of the project, and obtain a complete result (Theorem 1.5.10).

As mentioned in Section 1.1, there are two phenomena which do not exist in the setting where the costs are some constants. That is, it is possible that the firm should never enter the project, and there are diverse exit decisions. Moreover, we provide an explicit solution of entry-exit decisions if the project is worthy to be invested in.

2
Entry-exit decisions with implementation delay

Summary: We analyze entry-exit decisions with implementation delay of a project, and provide closed-form expressions for optimal entry decision times, optimal exit decision times and the maximal expected present value of the project. The results in conventional research were obtained under the restriction that the sum of the entry cost and exit cost is nonnegative. In practice, we usually meet this sum is negative, so it is necessary to remove the restriction. If the sum is negative, there may exist two trigger prices of optimal entry decisions, which does not happen when the sum is nonnegative, and it is not optimal to enter and then immediately exit the project even though it is an arbitrage opportunity.

2.1 Introduction

In practice, a major characteristic of investments is that there exist lags between decision times and corresponding implementation times. Some authors discussed entry-exit decision problems with implementation delay. For example, see [3, 15, 23, 34].

In [3], Bar-Ilan and Strange embedded lags in the classic model presented by Dixit[18]. They considered entry-exit decisions by employing the real option theory and derived a system of equations (see Equations (22)–(25) in [3]), then obtained semi-closed solutions for entry and exit decisions. However, they did not prove the existence and uniqueness of the solution to the system. Gauthier and Morellec[23] provided more explicit solutions through assuming *a priori* the forms of decision times. In [34], Øksendal studied two optimal exit decision problems with implementation delay—an assets selling problem and a resource extraction problem. In [15], Costeniuc *et al.* applied the probabilistic approach to entry-exit decisions with Parisian implementation delay from the view of real options.

The results in conventional research were obtained under the assumption that the sum of the entry cost and exit cost is nonnegative. In practice, we usually meet this sum is negative. For example, an investor buys a project at a low price and then sells it at a high price. We will remove this assumption and study the case where the sum is negative.

If the sum is nonnegative, there exists no arbitrage opportunity, and there is only one trigger price of entry decision. However, if the sum is negative, it is an arbitrage opportunity to enter and then immediately exit the project, and there may be two trigger prices of entry decision (⑥ of Theorem 2.5.6). We find that it is not optimal to enter and then immediately exit the project even if the sum is negative (see ③, ⑤ and ⑥ of Theorem 2.5.6 and Theorem 2.5.11).

In this chapter, we employ a method from the perspective of the optimal stopping theory, which proves to be natural, to rigorously discuss the entry-exit decision problem with implementation delay. We study this problem by three steps. First, we transform the delayed implementation case into an immediate implementation case. Second, we decompose the immediate implementation case into two standard optimal stopping problems, and then solve these two problems. Finally, we provide explicitly an optimal entry decision time, an optimal exit decision time and an expression of the maximal expected present value of the project.

We outline the structure of this chapter. In Section 2.2, we recall briefly the classical optimal stopping theory. In Section 2.3, we show that delayed optimal stopping problems involving two stopping times can be transformed to immediate stopping ones. In Section 2.4, we describe the model in detail. In Section 2.5, we obtain an optimal entry-exit decision as to when the firm decides to enter the project and when the firm decides to exit the project (Theorems 2.5.1 and 2.5.11).

2.2 Some results concerning classical optimal stopping problems

In this section, we recall briefly some results of classical optimal stopping problems. For details, we refer to [36, section 5.2].

Let $(\Omega, \mathscr{F}, \{\mathscr{F}_t\}_{t\geq 0}, \mathbb{P})$ be a filtered probability space with $\{\mathscr{F}_t\}_{t\geq 0}$ satisfying the usual conditions and $\mathscr{F}_0$ being the completion of $\{\emptyset, \Omega\}$. Let $B = (B(t), t \geq 0)$ be a d-dimensional standard Brownian motion defined on $(\Omega, \mathscr{F}, \{\mathscr{F}_t\}_{t\geq 0}, \mathbb{P})$.

Let $X = (X(t), t \geq 0)$ be a diffusion in $\mathbb{R}^n$ given by

$$\mathrm{d}X(t) = \alpha(X(t))\mathrm{d}t + \beta(X(t))\mathrm{d}B(t), \quad X(0) = x,$$

where $\alpha : \mathbb{R}^n \to \mathbb{R}^n$ and $\beta : \mathbb{R}^n \to \mathbb{R}^{n\times d}$ are some Lipschitz functions.

Let $\mathcal{T}$ denote the set of all stopping times valued in $[0, +\infty]$.

Theorem 2.2.1 *Consider the optimal stopping problem*

$$V(x) := \sup_{\tau\in\mathcal{T}} \mathbb{E}^x \left[\int_0^\tau \exp(-rt)f(X(t))\mathrm{d}t + \exp(-r\tau)g(X(\tau))\right] \tag{2.2.1}$$

for some Lipschitz functions f and g. Here, $\mathbb{E}^x[\ \cdot\ ] := \mathbb{E}[\ \cdot\ |X(0) = x]$, and $\exp(-r\tau)g(X(\tau)) \equiv 0$ on $\{\tau = +\infty\}$.

Assume that $r > 0$ is large enough. Then the following are true.

① *The value function V is Lipschitz continuous and is the unique viscosity solution with linear growth of the variational inequality*

$$\min\{rV - \mathcal{L}V - f, V - g\} = 0,$$

where $\mathcal{L}$ is the infinitesimal generator of X.

② *Set $\mathcal{S} := \{x : x \in \mathbb{R}^n, V(x) = g(x)\}$ which is called the exercise region. Then $\tau^* := \inf\{t : t > 0, X(t) \in \mathcal{S}\}$ is a maximizer of the problem (2.2.1).*

③ *The value function V is a viscosity solution of*

$$rV - \mathcal{L}V - f = 0 \qquad on \ \mathcal{C},$$

where $\mathcal{C} := \{x : x \in \mathbb{R}^n, V(x) > g(x)\}$ is the continuation region; moreover, if $\mathcal{L}$ is locally uniformly elliptic, V is C^2 on $\mathcal{C}$.

④ *Assume that X is 1-dimensional, $\mathcal{L}$ is locally uniformly elliptic, and g is C^1 on $\mathcal{S}$. Then V is C^1 on $\partial\mathcal{C}$ and C^2 at the isolated points of $\mathcal{S}$.*

⑤ *Define a function $\widehat{V}$ by*

$$\widehat{V}(x) := \mathbb{E}\left[\int_0^{+\infty} \exp(-rt) f(X(t))\mathrm{d}t\right].$$

Then $\mathcal{S} = \emptyset$ implies $\widehat{V} \geq g$ and $\widehat{V} \geq g$ implies $V = \widehat{V}$.

⑥ *If g is C^2 continuous on some open set $\mathcal{O}$, then $\mathcal{S} \subset \{x : x \in \mathcal{O}, rg(x) - \mathcal{L}g(x) - f(x) \geq 0\} \cup \mathcal{O}^c$, where $\mathcal{O}^c$ denotes the complement of $\mathcal{O}$ in $\mathbb{R}^n$.*

⑦ *Assume that X is 1-dimensional and takes values in $(0, +\infty)$, $X(t, x) \to X(t, 0) = 0$ as $x \to 0$, $\widehat{V}(x_0) < g(x_0)$ for some $x_0 > 0$, and g is C^2 continuous. We have the following two facts. If $\mathcal{D} = [a, +\infty)$ for some $a > 0$, where $\mathcal{D} := \{x : x > 0, rg(x) - \mathcal{L}g(x) - f(x) \geq 0\}$, then $\mathcal{S} = [x^*, +\infty)$ for some $x^* \in [a, +\infty)$. If $g(0) \geq f(0)/r$ and $\mathcal{D} = (0, a]$ for some $a > 0$, then $\mathcal{S} = (0, x^*]$ for some $x^* \in (0, a]$.*

Proof. We refer to [36, section 5.2] for the proof. □

2.3 A useful transformation

In this section, we show that delayed optimal stopping problems involving two stopping times can be transformed to immediate stopping ones. The proof is similar to that of [35, p. 38, Theorem 2.11].

Theorem 2.3.1 *Let δ be a nonnegative number. Consider the following two optimal stopping problems:*

(2.3.1)

$$J(x) := \sup_{\substack{\tau_1, \tau_2 \in \mathcal{T}, \\ \tau_1 \leq \tau_2}} \mathbb{E}^x\left[\int_{\tau_1+\delta}^{\tau_2+\delta} f(X(t))\mathrm{d}t + g_1(X(\tau_1 + \delta)) + g_2(X(\tau_2 + \delta))\right],$$

where $f, g_1, g_2 : \mathbb{R}^n \to \mathbb{R}$ *are three functions such that the expectations are finite;*

$$\text{(2.3.2)} \qquad \widetilde{J}(x) := \sup_{\substack{\tau_1,\tau_2 \in \mathcal{T}, \\ \tau_1 \le \tau_2}} \mathbb{E}^x \left[\int_{\tau_1}^{\tau_2} f(X(t))\mathrm{d}t + g_1^\delta(X(\tau_1)) + g_2^\delta(X(\tau_2)) \right],$$

where

$$g_1^\delta(x) := \mathbb{E}^x \left[-\int_0^\delta f(X(t))\mathrm{d}t + g_1(X(\delta)) \right],$$

and

$$g_2^\delta(x) := \mathbb{E}^x \left[\int_0^\delta f(X(t))\mathrm{d}t + g_2(X(\delta)) \right].$$

Then $J(x) = \widetilde{J}(x)$. *In addition, if* (τ_1^*, τ_2^*) *is a maximizer of* (2.3.2), *it is also a maximizer of* (2.3.1).

Proof. 1. Note that

$$\begin{aligned}
&\mathbb{E}^x \left[\int_{\tau_1+\delta}^{\tau_2+\delta} f(X(t))\mathrm{d}t + g_1(X(\tau_1+\delta)) + g_2(X(\tau_2+\delta)) \right] \\
&= \mathbb{E}^x \Bigg[\left(\int_{\tau_1}^{\tau_2} - \int_{\tau_1}^{\tau_1+\delta} + \int_{\tau_2}^{\tau_2+\delta} \right) f(X(t))\mathrm{d}t + \\
&\quad g_1(X(\tau_1+\delta)) + g_2(X(\tau_2+\delta)) \Bigg] \\
&= \mathbb{E}^x \Bigg[\int_{\tau_1}^{\tau_2} f(X(t))\mathrm{d}t - \int_{\tau_1}^{\tau_1+\delta} f(X(t))\mathrm{d}t + g_1(X(\tau_1+\delta)) + \\
&\quad \int_{\tau_2}^{\tau_2+\delta} f(X(t))\mathrm{d}t + g_2(X(\tau_2+\delta)) \Bigg].
\end{aligned}$$

Then, by the strong Markov property of the process X, we get

$$\begin{aligned}
&\mathbb{E}^x \left[\int_{\tau_1+\delta}^{\tau_2+\delta} f(X(t))\mathrm{d}t + g_1(X(\tau_1+\delta)) + g_2(X(\tau_2+\delta)) \right] \\
&= \mathbb{E}^x \Bigg[\int_{\tau_1}^{\tau_2} f(X(t))\mathrm{d}t + \mathbb{E}^{X(\tau_1)} \left[-\int_0^\delta f(X(t))\mathrm{d}t + g_1(X(\delta)) \right] + \\
&\quad \mathbb{E}^{X(\tau_2)} \left[\int_0^\delta f(X(t))\mathrm{d}t + g_2(X(\delta)) \right] \Bigg] \\
&= \mathbb{E}^x \left[\int_{\tau_1}^{\tau_2} f(X(t))\mathrm{d}t + g_1^\delta(X(\tau_1)) + g_2^\delta(X(\tau_2)) \right],
\end{aligned}$$

which completes the proof. □

2.4 The model

We return to entry-exit decision problems with implementation delay. Assume that the price process P follows

$$\mathrm{d}P(t) = \mu P(t)\mathrm{d}t + \sigma P(t)\mathrm{d}B(t), \text{ and } P(0) > 0, \tag{2.4.1}$$

where $\mu \in \mathbb{R}$, $\sigma > 0$, and B is a one dimensional standard Brownian motion, which denotes uncertainty.

Applying Itô's formula, we deduce that the solution of the equation (2.4.1) is

$$P(t) = P(0) \exp\left[\left(\mu - \frac{1}{2}\sigma^2\right) t + \sigma B(t)\right]. \tag{2.4.2}$$

To answer the questions—what time is optimal to make an entry (exit) decision, we will solve the optimal problem

(2.4.3)

$$J(p) := \sup_{\tau_I \leq \tau_O} \mathbb{E}^p\left[\int_{\tau_I+\delta}^{\tau_O+\delta} \exp(-rt)(P(t) - C)\mathrm{d}t - \exp(-r(\tau_I + \delta))K_I - \exp(-r(\tau_O + \delta))K_O\right],$$

where τ_I and τ_O are stopping times, r is the discount rate such that $r > 0$, C is the running cost, K_I is the entry cost, K_O is the exit cost, and the nonnegative number δ is a time lag between decision times and corresponding implementation times. We call stopping times τ_I and τ_O entry decision times and exit decision times, respectively, and the function J the maximal expected present value of the project.

Remark 2.4.1 (1) We do not propose any restriction on the costs, except that they are constant.

(2) Note that for any stopping time τ and nonnegative number δ, $\tau + \delta$ is also a stopping time. The maximal expected present value J of the delayed implementation case is no more than that of the corresponding immediate implementation case. We may interpret their difference as the loss due to delayed implementation.

(3) Furthermore, let $0 \leq \delta_1 < \delta_2 < +\infty$ and $\mathcal{T}$ is the collection of all stopping times, then $\{\tau + \delta_2 : \tau \in \mathcal{T}\} \subset \{\tau + \delta_1 : \tau \in \mathcal{T}\}$, thus the value of J corresponding to δ_2 is no more than that corresponding to δ_1. This implies the following principle: *once one has made a right decision, he/she should activate it as soon as possible.*

2.5 An optimal entry-exit decision

In this section, we provide an optimal entry-exit decision and an explicit expression for the function J.

Let us first consider a simple case $r \leq \mu$. In this case, noting the expression (2.4.2) of P, we have

$$\begin{aligned}
&\mathbb{E}^p\left[\int_\delta^{+\infty} \exp(-rt)(P(t) - C)\mathrm{d}t\right] \\
&= \int_\delta^{+\infty} \exp(-rt)\left[p\exp(\mu t) - C\right]\mathrm{d}t \\
&= \begin{cases} \lim\limits_{t\to+\infty}\left\{p(t-\delta) + \dfrac{C}{r}\left[\exp(-rt) - \exp(-r\delta)\right]\right\}, & \text{if } r = \mu, \\ \lim\limits_{t\to+\infty}\left\{\dfrac{p}{\mu - r}\left\{\exp[(\mu - r)t] - \exp[(\mu - r)\delta]\right\} + \right. \\ \qquad \left.\dfrac{C}{r}\left[\exp(-rt) - \exp(-r\delta)\right]\right\}, & \text{if } r < \mu \end{cases} \\
&= +\infty,
\end{aligned}$$

where we have used the fact that the process

$$\left(\exp\left(-\frac{1}{2}\sigma^2 t + \sigma B(t)\right), t \geq 0\right)$$

is a martingale (see [1, p. 288, Corollary 5.2.2]) for the first step.

Thus we obtain the following result.

Theorem 2.5.1 *Assume that $r \leq \mu$. Then $\tau_I^* := 0$ a.s. is an optimal entry decision time and $\tau_O^* := +\infty$ a.s. is an optimal exit decision time, i.e., the firm should never exit the project. In addition, the function J in (2.4.3) is given by $J \equiv +\infty$.*

Now we determine an optimal entry-exit decision for the case $r > \mu$. To this end, we first employ Theorem 2.3.1 to transform the delayed optimal stopping problem (2.4.3) to an immediate stopping one.

Theorem 2.5.2 *The delayed optimal stopping problem* (2.4.3) *is equivalent to the following optimal stopping problem:*

(2.5.1)

$$\widetilde{J}(p) := \sup_{\tau_I \leq \tau_O} \mathbb{E}^p \left[\int_{\tau_I}^{\tau_O} \exp(-rt)(P(t) - C)\mathrm{d}t - \exp(-r\tau_I)(k_1 P(\tau_I) + k_0) - \right.$$
$$\left. \exp(-r\tau_O)(l_1 P(\tau_O) + l_0) \right],$$

where

$$k_1 := \frac{\exp[(\mu - r)\delta] - 1}{\mu - r}, \quad k_0 := \frac{C}{r}[\exp(-r\delta) - 1] + \exp(-r\delta)K_I,$$
$$l_1 := -\frac{\exp[(\mu - r)\delta] - 1}{\mu - r}, \quad l_0 := -\frac{C}{r}[\exp(-r\delta) - 1] + \exp(-r\delta)K_O.$$

Proof. (1) Define a process X by $X(t) := [s + t, P(t)]^{\mathrm{T}}$, where $s \in \mathbb{R}$. Then

$$\mathrm{d}X(t) = \begin{bmatrix} 1 \\ \mu P(t) \end{bmatrix} \mathrm{d}t + \begin{bmatrix} 0 \\ \sigma P(t) \end{bmatrix} \mathrm{d}B(t), \quad X(0) = \begin{bmatrix} s \\ p \end{bmatrix}.$$

(2) According to Theorem 2.3.1, we need to calculate

$$\mathbb{E}^p \left[-\int_0^\delta \exp[-r(s+t)]\,(P(t) - C)\,\mathrm{d}t - \exp[-r(s+\delta)]K_I \right] \tag{2.5.2}$$

and

$$\mathbb{E}^p \left[\int_0^\delta \exp[-r(s+t)]\,(P(t) - C)\,\mathrm{d}t - \exp[-r(s+\delta)]K_O \right]. \tag{2.5.3}$$

For (2.5.2), we have

$$\mathbb{E}^p \left[-\int_0^\delta \exp[-r(s+t)]\,(P(t) - C)\,\mathrm{d}t - \exp[-r(s+\delta)]K_I \right]$$
$$= -\int_0^\delta \exp[-r(s+t)]\,[p\exp(\mu t) - C]\,\mathrm{d}t - \exp[-r(s+\delta)]K_I$$
$$= -\exp(-rs)\left\{ \frac{p}{\mu - r}\,\{\exp[(\mu - r)\delta] - 1\} + \right.$$
$$\left. \frac{C}{r}\,[\exp(-r\delta) - 1] + \exp(-r\delta)K_I \right\},$$

where we have used the fact that the process

$$\left(\exp\left(-\frac{1}{2}\sigma^2 t + \sigma B(t)\right), t \geq 0\right)$$

is a martingale (see [1, p. 288, Corollary 5.2.2]) for the first step.

Similarly, we can calculate (2.5.3). Therefore, in light of Theorem 2.3.1, the delayed optimal stopping problem (2.4.3) is equivalent to the optimal stopping problem (2.5.1). □

In order to solve the optimal stopping problem (2.5.1), we will solve the following two optimal stopping problems:

(2.5.4)
$$G(p) := \sup_{\tau_O} \mathbb{E}^p \left[\int_0^{\tau_O} \exp(-rt)(P(t) - C)\mathrm{d}t - \exp(-r\tau_O)(l_1 P(\tau_O) + l_0)\right]$$

and

(2.5.5)
$$H(p) := \sup_{\tau_I} \mathbb{E}^p \left[\exp(-r\tau_I)\left(G(P(\tau_I)) - k_1 P(\tau_I) - k_0\right)\right].$$

Assume that $r > \mu$. Let λ_1 and λ_2 be the solutions of the quadratic equation

$$r - \mu\lambda - \frac{1}{2}\sigma^2\lambda(\lambda - 1) = 0$$

with $\lambda_1 < \lambda_2$. Then we have $\lambda_1 < 0$ and $\lambda_2 > 1$.

Theorem 2.5.3 *For the optimal stopping problem* (2.5.4), *the following are true.*

① *If $r > \mu$ and $C \leq rK_O$, then $\tau_O^* := +\infty$ a.s. is a maximizer of* (2.5.4). *In addition, $G(p) = p/(r - \mu) - C/r$.*

② *If $r > \mu$ and $C > rK_O$, then $\tau_O^* := \inf\{t : t > 0, P(t) \leq p_O\}$ is a maximizer of* (2.5.4), *where*

$$p_O = \exp(-\mu\delta)\frac{\lambda_1}{\lambda_1 - 1}(r - \mu)\left(\frac{C}{r} - K_O\right).$$

In addition,

$$G(p) = \begin{cases} Ap^{\lambda_1} + \dfrac{p}{r - \mu} - \dfrac{C}{r}, & \text{if } p > p_O, \\ \dfrac{p}{\mu - r}\{\exp[(\mu - r)\delta] - 1\} + \\ \qquad \dfrac{C}{r}[\exp(-r\delta) - 1] - \exp(-r\delta)K_O, & \text{if } p \leq p_O, \end{cases}$$

where $A = \exp[(\mu - r)\delta]{p_O}^{1-\lambda_1}/[\lambda_1(\mu - r)]$.

Proof. (1) Assume that $r > \mu$ and $C \le rK_O$.

Noting that

$$\mathbb{E}^p\left[\int_0^{+\infty} \exp(-rt)(P(t) - C)\right] = \frac{p}{r - \mu} - \frac{C}{r},$$

we have

$$\mathbb{E}^p\left[\int_0^{+\infty} \exp(-rt)(P(t) - C)\right] \ge -l_1 p - l_0.$$

Therefore, by ⑤ of Theorem 2.2.1, we achieve ①.

(2) Assume that $r > \mu$ and $C > rK_O$.

In this case, we have $\mathcal{D} = (0, \exp(-\mu\delta)(C - rK_O)]$. Thus, by ⑦ of Theorem 2.2.1, the exercise region is of the form $(0, p_O]$ for some $p_O \in (0, +\infty)$. On the continuation region $(p_O, +\infty)$, G satisfies the equation

$$rG - \mu p G' - \frac{1}{2}\sigma^2 p^2 G'' - p + C = 0$$

by ③ of Theorem 2.2.1. Furthermore, by the Lipschitz property of G, we have

$$G(p) = Ap^{\lambda_1} + \frac{p}{r - \mu} - \frac{C}{r}$$

for some constant A.

Note that G is C^1 continuous at p_O by ④ of Theorem 2.2.1. We get the following system

$$\begin{cases} Ap_O^{\lambda_1} + \dfrac{p_O}{r-\mu} - \dfrac{C}{r} = \dfrac{p_O}{\mu - r}\{\exp[(\mu - r)\delta] - 1\} + \\ \qquad\qquad \dfrac{C}{r}[\exp(-r\delta) - 1] - \exp(-r\delta)K_O \\ \lambda_1 A p_O^{\lambda_1 - 1} + \dfrac{1}{r - \mu} = \dfrac{\exp[(\mu - r)\delta] - 1}{\mu - r}, \end{cases}$$

from which we obtain

$$p_O = \exp(-\mu\delta)\frac{\lambda_1}{\lambda_1 - 1}(r - \mu)\left(\frac{C}{r} - K_O\right) \tag{2.5.6}$$

and

$$A = \exp[(\mu - r)\delta]\frac{{p_O}^{1-\lambda_1}}{\lambda_1(\mu - r)}.$$

The proof is complete. □

Remark 2.5.4 We will prove in Theorem 2.5.11 that p_O is a trigger price of optimal exit decisions.

Corollary 2.5.5 *The optimal exit trigger price p_O in Theorem 2.5.3 satisfies $p_O < \exp(-\mu\delta)\,(C - rK_O)$.*

Proof. Note that $1/\lambda_1 < \mu/r$. Then, thanks to (2.5.6), the conclusion follows. □

Theorem 2.5.6 *For the optimal stopping problem (2.5.5), the following are true.*

① *If $r > \mu$, $C - rK_O \le 0$ and $C + rK_I \le 0$, then $\tau_I^* := 0$ a.s. is a maximizer of (2.5.5). In addition,*

$$H(p) = \frac{\exp[(\mu - r)\delta]}{r - \mu} p - \exp(-r\delta)\left(\frac{C}{r} + K_I\right).$$

② *If $r > \mu$, $C - rK_O \le 0$ and $C + rK_I > 0$, then $\tau_I^* := \inf\{t : t > 0, P(t) \ge p_I\}$ is a maximizer of (2.5.5), where*

$$p_I = \exp(-\mu\delta)\frac{\lambda_2}{\lambda_2 - 1}(r - \mu)\left(\frac{C}{r} + K_I\right).$$

In addition,

$$H(p) = \begin{cases} Bp^{\lambda_2}, & \text{if } p < p_I, \\ \dfrac{\exp[(\mu - r)\delta]}{r - \mu} p - \exp(-r\delta)\left(\dfrac{C}{r} + K_I\right), & \text{if } p \ge p_I, \end{cases}$$

where $B = \exp[(\mu - r)\delta]{p_I}^{1-\lambda_2}/[\lambda_2(r - \mu)]$.

③ *If $r > \mu$, $C - rK_O > 0$ and $C + rK_I \le 0$, then $\tau_I^* := 0$ a.s. is a maximizer of (2.5.5). In addition,*

$$H(p) = \begin{cases} Ap^{\lambda_1} + \dfrac{\exp[(\mu - r)\delta]}{r - \mu} p - \exp(-r\delta)\left(\dfrac{C}{r} + K_I\right), \\ \hfill \text{if } p > p_O, \\ -\exp(-r\delta)(K_I + K_O), \quad \text{if } p \le p_O. \end{cases}$$

④ *If* $r > \mu$, $C - rK_O > 0$, $C + rK_I > 0$ *and* $K_I + K_O \geq 0$, *then* $\tau_I^* := \inf\{t : t > 0, P(t) \geq p_I\}$ *is a maximizer of* (2.5.5), *where* p_I *is the largest solution of the algebraic equation*

$$A(\lambda_2 - \lambda_1)p_I^{\lambda_1} + \frac{\exp[(\mu - r)\delta]}{r - \mu}(\lambda_2 - 1)p_I - \lambda_2 \exp(-r\delta)\left(\frac{C}{r} + K_I\right) = 0.$$

In addition,

$$H(p) = \begin{cases} Bp^{\lambda_2}, & \text{if } p < p_I, \\ Ap^{\lambda_1} + \dfrac{\exp[(\mu - r)\delta]}{r - \mu}p - \exp(-r\delta)\left(\dfrac{C}{r} + K_I\right), & \text{if } p \geq p_I, \end{cases}$$

where

$$B = \lambda_1 \lambda_2^{-1} A p_I^{\lambda_1 - \lambda_2} + \exp[(\mu - r)\delta]\frac{{p_I}^{1-\lambda_2}}{\lambda_2(r - \mu)}.$$

⑤ *If* $r > \mu$, $C - rK_O > 0$, $C + rK_I > 0$, $K_I + K_O < 0$ *and* $p_O \geq \exp(-\mu\delta)(C + rK_I)$, *then* $\tau_I^* := 0$ *a.s. is a maximizer of* (2.5.5). *In addition,*

$$H(p) = \begin{cases} Ap^{\lambda_1} + \dfrac{\exp[(\mu - r)\delta]}{r - \mu}p - \exp(-r\delta)\left(\dfrac{C}{r} + K_I\right), & \text{if } p > p_O, \\ -\exp(-r\delta)(K_I + K_O), & \text{if } p \leq p_O. \end{cases}$$

⑥ *If* $r > \mu$, $C - rK_O > 0$, $C + rK_I > 0$, $K_I + K_O < 0$ *and* $p_O < \exp(-\mu\delta)(C + rK_I)$, *then* $\tau_I^* := \inf\{t : t > 0, P(t) \leq p_I^{(1)}$ *or* $P(t) \geq p_I^{(2)}\}$ *is a maximizer of* (2.5.5), *where* $(p_I^{(1)}, p_I^{(2)})$ *is the solution of the equation*

$$\begin{bmatrix} \lambda_2 p_I^{(1)^{-\lambda_1}} & -p_I^{(1)^{-\lambda_1}} \\ -\lambda_1 p_I^{(1)^{-\lambda_2}} & p_I^{(1)^{-\lambda_2}} \end{bmatrix} \begin{bmatrix} -\exp(-r\delta)(K_I + K_O) \\ 0 \end{bmatrix}$$

$$(2.5.7) \quad = \begin{bmatrix} \lambda_2 p_I^{(2)^{-\lambda_1}} & -p_I^{(2)^{-\lambda_1}} \\ -\lambda_1 p_I^{(2)^{-\lambda_2}} & p_I^{(2)^{-\lambda_2}} \end{bmatrix} \begin{bmatrix} Ap_I^{(2)^{\lambda_1}} + \dfrac{\exp[(\mu - r)\delta]}{r - \mu}p_I^{(2)} - \exp(-r\delta)\left(\dfrac{C}{r} + K_I\right) \\ \lambda_1 A p_I^{(2)^{\lambda_1}} + \dfrac{\exp[(\mu - r)\delta]}{r - \mu}p_I^{(2)} \end{bmatrix}$$

with $p_I^{(1)} < p_I^{(2)}$.
In addition,

$$H(p) = \begin{cases} Ap^{\lambda_1} + \dfrac{\exp[(\mu - r)\delta]}{r - \mu} p - \exp(-r\delta)\left(\dfrac{C}{r} + K_I\right), \\ \qquad\qquad\qquad\qquad\qquad\qquad\qquad\qquad \text{if } p \geq p_I^{(2)}, \\ B_1 p^{\lambda_1} + B_2 p^{\lambda_2}, \quad \text{if } p_I^{(1)} < p < p_I^{(2)}, \\ -\exp(-r\delta)(K_I + K_O), \quad \text{if } p \leq p_I^{(1)}, \end{cases}$$

where

$$B_1 = -\frac{\lambda_2 p_I^{(1)^{-\lambda_1}} \exp(-r\delta)}{\lambda_2 - \lambda_1}(K_I + K_O)$$

and

$$B_2 = \frac{\lambda_1 p_I^{(1)^{-\lambda_2}} \exp(-r\delta)}{\lambda_2 - \lambda_1}(K_I + K_O).$$

Proof. (1) Assume that $r > \mu$, $C - rK_O \leq 0$ and $C + rK_I \leq 0$.

Define a function w by

$$w(p) := \frac{\exp[(\mu - r)\delta]}{r - \mu} p - \exp(-r\delta)\left(\frac{C}{r} + K_I\right) \qquad \text{for } p \in (0, +\infty).$$

Then we have

$$rw(p) - \mu p w'(p) - \frac{1}{2}\sigma^2 p^2 w''(p) \geq 0,$$

which implies w is a viscosity solution of

$$\min\left\{rV - \mu p V' - \frac{1}{2}\sigma^2 p^2 V'', V - w\right\} = 0 \qquad \text{on } (0, +\infty).$$

Note that $H(0^+) = w(0^+)$. Thus, by the uniqueness of viscosity solutions (see ① of Theorem 2.2.1), we have $H(p) = w(p)$. Consequently, the exercise region is $(0, +\infty)$, i.e., $\tau_I^* := 0$ a.s. is a maximizer of (2.5.5) by ② of Theorem 2.2.1.

(2) Assume that $r > \mu$, $C - rK_O \leq 0$ and $C + rK_I > 0$.

In this case, we have $\mathcal{D} = [\exp(-\mu\delta)(C + rK_I), +\infty)$. Thus, by ⑦ of Theorem 2.2.1, the exercise region is of the form $[p_I, +\infty)$ for some $p_I \in (0, +\infty)$. On the continuation region $(0, p_I)$, H satisfies the equation

$$rH - \mu p H' - \frac{1}{2}\sigma^2 p^2 H'' = 0$$

by ③ of Theorem 2.2.1. Furthermore, by the Lipschitz property of H, we have $H(p) = Bp^{\lambda_2}$ for some constant B.

Note that H is C^1 continuous at p_I by ④ of Theorem 2.2.1. We get the following system

$$\begin{cases} Bp_I^{\lambda_2} = \dfrac{\exp[(\mu - r)\delta]}{r-\mu} p_I - \exp(-r\delta)\left(\dfrac{C}{r} + K_I\right) \\ \lambda_2 Bp_I^{\lambda_2 - 1} = \dfrac{\exp[(\mu - r)\delta]}{r-\mu}, \end{cases}$$

from which we obtain

$$p_I = \exp(-\mu\delta)\frac{\lambda_2}{\lambda_2 - 1}(r-\mu)\left(\frac{C}{r} + K_I\right)$$

and

$$B = \exp[(\mu - r)\delta]\frac{{p_I}^{1-\lambda_2}}{\lambda_2(r-\mu)}.$$

(3) Assume that $r > \mu$, $C - rK_O > 0$ and $C + rK_I \le 0$.

Define a function w by

$$w(p) := \begin{cases} Ap^{\lambda_1} + \dfrac{\exp[(\mu - r)\delta]}{r-\mu} p - \exp(-r\delta)\left(\dfrac{C}{r} + K_I\right), & \text{if } p > p_O, \\ -\exp(-r\delta)(K_I + K_O), & \text{if } p \le p_O. \end{cases}$$

Then w is a viscosity subsolution of

$$\min\left\{rV - \mu pV' - \frac{1}{2}\sigma^2 p^2 V'', V - w\right\} = 0 \quad \text{on } (0, +\infty). \tag{2.5.8}$$

We prove that w is a viscosity supersolution of (2.5.8). To this end, we only need to prove

$$rw(p_O) - \mu p\varphi'(p_O) - \frac{1}{2}\sigma^2 p^2 \varphi''(p_O) \ge 0 \tag{2.5.9}$$

for any function $\varphi \in C^2(\mathcal{N}(p_O))$ such that $w(p_O) = \varphi(p_O)$ and $w(p) \ge \varphi(p)$ on some neighbourhood $\mathcal{N}(p_O)$ of p_O, since $rw - \mu pw' - \sigma^2 p^2 w''/2 \ge 0$ on $(0, p_O) \cup (p_O + \infty)$.

Noting that p_O is a minimizer of $w - \varphi$ on $\mathcal{N}(p_O)$, we have $w'(p_O) - \varphi'(p_O) = 0$ and $w''_-(p_O) - \varphi''(p_O) \ge 0$, i.e., $\varphi'(p_O) = 0$ and $\varphi''(p_O) \le 0$. In addition, thanks to $C - rK_O > 0$ and $C + rK_I \le 0$, $K_I + K_O < 0$. So (2.5.9) holds.

In summery, w is a viscosity solution of

$$\min\left\{rV - \mu pV' - \frac{1}{2}\sigma^2 p^2 V'', V - w\right\} = 0 \qquad \text{on } (0, +\infty).$$

Note that $H(0^+) = w(0^+)$. Then, by the uniqueness of viscosity solutions (see ① of Theorem 2.2.1), we get $H(p) = w(p)$ for $p \in (0, +\infty)$. Consequently, the exercise region is $(0, +\infty)$, i.e., $\tau_I^* := 0$ a.s. is a maximizer of (2.5.5) by ② of Theorem 2.2.1.

(4) Assume that $r > \mu$, $C - rK_O > 0$, $C + rK_I > 0$ and $K_I + K_O \geq 0$.

First assume $K_I + K_O > 0$. Then, in light of ⑥ of Theorem 2.2.1, we have

$$\mathcal{S} \subset [\exp(-\mu\delta)(C + rK_I), +\infty) \cup \{p_O\}.$$

Note that $p_O < \exp(-\mu\delta)(C - rK_O)$ by Corollary 2.5.5, and $K_I + K_O > 0$. These imply $p_O < \exp(-\mu\delta)(C + rK_I)$. Consequently, by following the proof of ⑦ of Theorem 2.2.1 (see [36, p. 104]) and using ④ of Theorem 2.2.1, there is a point $p_I \in [\exp(-\mu\delta)(C + rK_I), +\infty)$ such that

$$H(p) = G(p) - k_1 p - k_0 \qquad \text{for } p \in [p_I, +\infty)$$

and

$$rH - \mu pH' - \frac{1}{2}\sigma^2 p^2 H'' = 0 \qquad \text{on } (0, p_I). \tag{2.5.10}$$

Thus, by the Lipschitz property of H, we have $H(p) = Bp^{\lambda_2}$ for some constant B from (2.5.10).

Note that H is C^1 continuous at p_I by ④ of Theorem 2.2.1. We get the following system:

$$\begin{cases} Bp_I^{\lambda_2} = Ap_I^{\lambda_1} + \dfrac{\exp[(\mu - r)\delta]}{r - \mu} p_I - \exp(-r\delta)\left(\dfrac{C}{r} + K_I\right) \\ \lambda_2 B p_I^{\lambda_2 - 1} = \lambda_1 A p_I^{\lambda_1 - 1} + \dfrac{\exp[(\mu - r)\delta]}{r - \mu}, \end{cases} \tag{2.5.11}$$

from which we obtain

$$A(\lambda_2 - \lambda_1)p_I^{\lambda_1} + \frac{\exp[(\mu - r)\delta]}{r - \mu}(\lambda_2 - 1)p_I - \lambda_2 \exp(-r\delta)\left(\frac{C}{r} + K_I\right) = 0.$$

We will show ahead in Lemma 2.5.9 that the above algebraic equation has only two roots. One is less than p_O, and the other is greater than p_O. Since $p_I \geq \exp(-\mu\delta)(C + rK_I)$, $p_O < \exp(-\mu\delta)(C - rK_O)$ by Corollary 2.5.5, and $K_I + K_O > 0$, we must choose the greater one. Furthermore, we have

$$B = \lambda_1 \lambda_2^{-1} A p_I^{\lambda_1 - \lambda_2} + \exp[(\mu - r)\delta] \frac{{p_I}^{1-\lambda_2}}{\lambda_2 (r - \mu)}.$$

For proving the exercise region is $[p_I, +\infty)$, we only need to show

$$H(p_O) > G(p_O) - k_1 p_O - k_0. \tag{2.5.12}$$

To see this, consider the function $f(p) := H(p) - G(p) + k_1 p + k_0$ for $p \in [0, p_O]$. Then we have $f(0) = \exp(-r\delta)(K_I + K_O) > 0$. In addition, $f'(p) = \lambda_2 B p^{\lambda_2 - 1} > 0$ for $p \in (0, p_O)$, since $B > 0$ by (2.5.11) and Lemma 2.5.9. The inequality (2.5.12) follows.

Now consider the case $K_I + K_O = 0$. We refer to the following Step 6. To solve the systems (2.5.13) and (2.5.14), we put $B_1 = p_I^{(1)} = 0$, then the systems (2.5.13) and (2.5.14) are reduced to (2.5.11). By repeating the proof of the case $K_I + K_O > 0$, we achieve our aim.

(5) Assume that $r > \mu$, $C - rK_O > 0$, $C + rK_I > 0$, $K_I + K_O < 0$ and $p_O \geq \exp(-\mu\delta)(C + rK_I)$. The proof of this case is the same as that of the case ③.

(6) Assume that $r > \mu$, $C - rK_O > 0$, $C + rK_I > 0$, $K_I + K_O < 0$ and $p_O < \exp(-\mu\delta)(C + rK_I)$.

In this case, we have

$$\mathcal{S} \subset (0, p_O] \cup [\exp(-\mu\delta)(C + rK_I), +\infty).$$

Thus, by following the proof of ⑦ of Theorem 2.2.1 (see [36, p. 104]), the exercise region is of the form $(0, p_I^{(1)}] \cup [p_I^{(2)}, +\infty)$ for some $p_I^{(1)} \in (0, p_O]$ and $p_I^{(2)} \in [\exp(-\mu\delta)(C + rK_I), +\infty)$. On the continuation region $(p_I^{(1)}, p_I^{(2)})$, H satisfies the equation

$$rH - \mu p H' - \frac{1}{2}\sigma^2 p^2 H'' = 0$$

by ③ of Theorem 2.2.1.

Thus we have $H(p) = B_1 p^{\lambda_1} + B_2 p^{\lambda_2}$ on $(p_I^{(1)}, p_I^{(2)})$ for some constants B_1 and B_2.

Note that H is C^1 continuous at $p_I^{(1)}$ and $p_I^{(2)}$ by ④ of Theorem 2.2.1. We get the following systems:

$$(2.5.13) \qquad \begin{cases} B_1 p_I^{(1)\lambda_1} + B_2 p_I^{(1)\lambda_2} = -\exp(-r\delta)(K_I + K_O) \\ \lambda_1 B_1 p_I^{(1)\lambda_1 - 1} + \lambda_2 B_2 p_I^{(1)\lambda_2 - 1} = 0 \end{cases}$$

and

$$(2.5.14) \qquad \begin{cases} B_1 p_I^{(2)\lambda_1} + B_2 p_I^{(2)\lambda_2} = A p_I^{(2)\lambda_1} + \dfrac{\exp[(\mu - r)\delta]}{r-\mu} p_I^{(2)} - \\ \qquad\qquad \exp(-r\delta)\left(\dfrac{C}{r} + K_I\right) \\ \lambda_1 B_1 p_I^{(2)\lambda_1 - 1} + \lambda_2 B_2 p_I^{(2)\lambda_2 - 1} = \lambda_1 A p_I^{(2)\lambda_1 - 1} + \dfrac{\exp[(\mu - r)\delta]}{r-\mu}, \end{cases}$$

from which, by solving B_1 and B_2, respectively, we obtain (2.5.7). □

Remark 2.5.7 We will prove in Theorem 2.5.11 that p_I, $p_I^{(1)}$ and $p_I^{(2)}$ are trigger prices of optimal entry decisions.

Corollary 2.5.8 *The optimal entry trigger prices* p_I *in* ② *and* ④ *of Theorem* 2.5.6 *satisfy* $p_I > \exp(-\mu\delta)(C + rK_I)$*; the optimal entry trigger prices* $p_I^{(1)}$ *and* $p_I^{(2)}$ *in* ⑥ *of Theorem* 2.5.6 *satisfy* $p_I^{(1)} < \exp(-\mu\delta)(C - rK_O)$ *and* $p_I^{(2)} > \exp(-\mu\delta)(C + rK_I)$*, respectively.*

Proof. (1) For the case ② of Theorem 2.5.6, we have

$$p_I = \exp(-\mu\delta)\frac{\lambda_2}{\lambda_2 - 1}(r - \mu)\left(\frac{C}{r} + K_I\right).$$

In addition, note that $1/\lambda_2 > \mu/r$. The inequality $p_I > \exp(-\mu\delta)(C + rK_I)$ follows.

(2) Consider the case ④ of Theorem 2.5.6.

Define a function U by

$$U(p) := Bp^{\lambda_2} - G(p) + k_1 p + k_0 \qquad \text{for } p \in [p_O, +\infty).$$

Then we have $U(p_O) \geq 0$ and $U(p_I) = 0$.

We prove the equation $U''(p)=0$ has a solution in (p_O, p_I). To this end, suppose that the equation $U''(p)=0$ has no solution in (p_O, p_I). Then the function $U'(\cdot)$ is strictly monotonous on $[p_O, p_I]$. In addition, note that $U'(p_O)=\lambda_2 B p_O^{\lambda_2-1}>0$ and $U'(p_I)=0$. We get $U'(p)>0$ for $p_O<p<p_I$. Consequently, $0\le U(p_O)<U(p_I)=0$, which is a contradiction.

On the other hand, by noting $U''(p)=\lambda_2(\lambda_2-1)Bp^{\lambda_2-2}-\lambda_1(\lambda_1-1)Ap^{\lambda_1-2}$, the equation $U''(p)=0$ has at most one solution in $(p_O,+\infty)$.

Therefore, $U''(p_I)>0$, and then

$$\begin{aligned}&r(G(p_I)-k_1p_I-k_0)-\mu p_I(G'(p_I)-k_1)-\frac{1}{2}\sigma^2p_I^2G''(p_I)\\ &>rH(p_I)-\mu p_IH'(p_I)-\frac{1}{2}\sigma^2p_I^2H''_-(p_I)=0,\end{aligned}$$

i.e.,

$$p_I>\exp(-\mu\delta)(C+rK_I),$$

where we have used $rG(p_I)-\mu p_IG'(p_I)-\sigma^2p_I^2G''(p_I)/2=p_I-C$.

(3) The inequality $p_I^{(1)}<\exp(-\mu\delta)(C-rK_O)$ follows from $p_I^{(1)}\le p_O$ and Corollary 2.5.5. The proof of the inequality $p_I^{(2)}>\exp(-\mu\delta)(C+rK_I)$ is similar to Step 2. □

Lemma 2.5.9 *Assume that* $r>\mu$, $C-rK_O>0$, $C+rK_I>0$ *and* $K_I+K_O\ge 0$. *Then the equation*

$$A(\lambda_2-\lambda_1)p^{\lambda_1}+\frac{\exp[(\mu-r)\delta]}{r-\mu}(\lambda_2-1)p-\lambda_2\exp(-r\delta)\left(\frac{C}{r}+K_I\right)=0$$

has only two solutions p_1 *and* p_2 *in* $(0,+\infty)$ *satisfying* $p_1\le p_O$ *and* $p_2>p_O$. *Furthermore,* $\lambda_1Ap_2^{\lambda_1}+\exp[(\mu-r)\delta]/(r-\mu)>0$.

Proof. The proof is similar to that of Lemma 1.5.6.

(1) Defined a function E by

$$E(p):=A(\lambda_2-\lambda_1)p^{\lambda_1}+\frac{\exp[(\mu-r)\delta]}{r-\mu}(\lambda_2-1)p-\lambda_2\exp(-r\delta)\left(\frac{C}{r}+K_I\right).$$

Suppose that the equation $E(p)=0$ has three solutions in $(0,+\infty)$. Then by Rolle's mean value theorem, there is a positive number ξ such that $E''(\xi)=0$, i.e.,

$$A(\lambda_2-\lambda_1)\lambda_1(\lambda_1-1)\xi^{\lambda_1-2}=0,$$

which is impossible. Thus the equation $E(p) = 0$ has at most two solutions in $(0, +\infty)$.

(2) In this step, we will estimate $E(p_O)$ and $E'(p_O)$.

We first estimate $E(p_O)$ as follows.

$$\begin{aligned} E(p_O) = &(\lambda_2 - \lambda_1)\left\{\frac{\exp[(\mu - r)\delta]}{\mu - r}p_O + \exp(-r\delta)\left(\frac{C}{r} - K_O\right)\right\} + \\ &\frac{\exp[(\mu - r)\delta]}{r - \mu}(\lambda_2 - 1)p_O - \lambda_2 \exp(-r\delta)\left(\frac{C}{r} + K_I\right) \\ = &-\lambda_2 \exp(-r\delta)(K_I + K_O) \leq 0, \end{aligned}$$

where we have used the continuity of the function G at p_O for the first equality.

Now we estimate $E'(p_O)$.

$$\begin{aligned} E'(p_O) &= (\lambda_1 - \lambda_2)\frac{\exp[(\mu - r)\delta]}{r - \mu} + (\lambda_2 - 1)\frac{\exp[(\mu - r)\delta]}{r - \mu} \\ &= (\lambda_1 - 1)\frac{\exp[(\mu - r)\delta]}{r - \mu} < 0, \end{aligned}$$

where we have used the C^1 continuity of the function G at p_O for the first equality.

(3) Note that $\lim_{p \to 0^+} E(p) = +\infty$, $\lim_{p \to +\infty} E(p) = +\infty$, $E(p_O) \leq 0$ and $E'(p_O) < 0$. We find that the equation $E(p) = 0$ has only two solutions p_1 and p_2 in $(0, +\infty)$ satisfying $p_1 \leq p_O$ and $p_2 > p_O$.

Furthermore, $E'(p_2) > 0$. It follows that

$$\begin{aligned} \lambda_1 A p_2^{\lambda_1} + \frac{\exp[(\mu - r)\delta]}{r - \mu} &> \lambda_1 A p_2^{\lambda_1} + \frac{\lambda_2 - 1}{\lambda_2 - \lambda_1} \times \frac{\exp[(\mu - r)\delta]}{r - \mu} \\ &= \frac{1}{\lambda_2 - \lambda_1} E'(p_2) > 0. \end{aligned}$$

The proof is complete. □

Recall the problem (2.4.3). The following Theorem 2.5.11 provides a solution to entry and exit decisions and an explicit expression for the maximal expected present value of the project. To prove Theorem 2.5.11, we need the following lemma.

Lemma 2.5.10 (cf. Lemma 1.4.1) *Assume that* $r > \mu$. *Then the family of random variables* $\{\exp[(\mu - r - \sigma^2/2)\tau + \sigma B(\tau)] : \tau \in \mathcal{T}\}$ *is uniformly integrable, where* $\mathcal{T}$ *is the collection of all stopping times.*

Theorem 2.5.11 *In each case of Theorem 2.5.6,* τ_I^* *is an optimal entry decision time, and* τ_O^* *is an optimal exit decision time, where* $\tau_O^* := +\infty$ *a.s. if* $C \leq rK_O$ *and* $\tau_O^* := \inf\{t : t > \tau_I^*$ *and* $P(t) \leq p_O\}$ *if* $C > rK_O$*, respectively. In addition, we have* $J(p) = H(p)$.

Proof. (1) Recall the problem (2.5.1)

$$\widetilde{J}(p) := \sup_{\tau_I \leq \tau_O} \mathbb{E}^p \left[\int_{\tau_I}^{\tau_O} \exp(-rt)(P(t) - C)\mathrm{d}t - \exp(-r\tau_I)(k_1 P(\tau_I) + k_0) - \exp(-r\tau_O)(l_1 P(\tau_O) + l_0) \right].$$

(2) Similar arguments to the proof of Theorem 1.5.10 show us that $\widetilde{J}(p) = H(p)$ and (τ_I^*, τ_O^*) is a solution of the problem (2.5.1). Consequently, These and Theorem 2.5.2 complete the proof. □

Example 2.5.12 Take $r = 0.2$, $\mu = 0.1$, $\sigma = 0.3$, $\delta = 1$, $C = 10$, $K_I = -20$ and $K_O = 10$. Then we have $r > \mu$, $C - rK_O > 0$, $C + rK_I > 0$, $K_I + K_O < 0$ and $p_O = 2.66841 < 5.42902 = \exp(-\mu\delta)(C + rK_I)$. Thus we apply ⑥ of Theorem 2.5.6, and get $p_I^{(1)} = 1.96101$ and $p_I^{(2)} = 6.94641$. Therefore, by Theorem 2.5.11, $\inf\{t : t > 0, P(t) \leq 1.96101$ or $P(t) \geq 6.94641\}$ is an optimal entry decision time and $\inf\{t : t > \tau_I^*, P(t) \leq 2.66841\}$ is an optimal exit decision time.

2.6 Conclusions

We have to face the fact that activating decisions is usually postponed. In this chapter, we study an entry-exit decision problem with delayed implementation. We first clarify it from the view of optimal stopping in Section 2.4, then discuss the trivial case in Theorem 2.5.1, and finally obtain an explicit solution in Theorem 2.5.11 for the nontrivial case.

The results in literature were obtained under the assumption that the sum of the entry cost and exit cost is nonnegative, which limits the application of the model (2.4.3). We here abandon the assumption. If the sum is negative, two trigger prices of optimal entry decisions may exist, which does not happen if the sum is nonnegative. Even though it is an arbitrage opportunity to enter a project and then exit it immediately if the sum is negative, it is still not advisable.

3
Entry-exit decisions with underlying processes following geometric Lévy processes

Summary: We study entry-exit decision problems of a project in the context that the log-price process follows a Lévy process with exponential jumps. A closed-form solution to the problems is obtained. To be specific, we show explicitly an optimal entry time, an optimal exit time and an expression of the maximal expected present value of the project. Moreover, it is also anatomized that how the jumping of the Lévy process affects optimal entry and exit times. While the negative effect of jumping on prices grows, the optimal exit time gets earlier, and the optimal entry time, however, first moves up and then moves down. In addition, the optimal exit time decreases with the frequency of jumps increasing when the negative effect dominates the positive effect, and increases when the opposite situation holds; the optimal entry time first increases and then decreases as the frequency becomes higher if the negative effect dominates the positive effect, and increases if the contrary condition is satisfied.

3.1 Introduction

In practice, a major characteristic of underlying processes is that they involve jumps. It is natural to regard them as some geometric Lévy processes.

Boyarchenko and Levendorskiĭ discussed in [6, Chapter 11] exit and entry decisions in some geometric Lévy process settings through the real option approach. Specifically, they considered an entry decision problem: if a project will be never abandoned once it is activated, what is the optimal time to activate it, and an exit decision problem: if a project is in activity, what is the optimal time to abandon it.

In this chapter, we analyze entry-exit decisions with underlying processes involving jumps. A firm intends to schedule a project which produces some commodity whose log-price follows a Lévy process with exponential jumps. The firm faces a problem, i.e., when starting the project and when ending it in order to gain the maximal expected profit. We model this decision problem from the viewpoint of optimal stopping theory.

We work out the answer to the problem by two steps. First, we reduce the problem to two standard optimal stopping problems, and then solve these two problems by means of Wiener-Hopf factorization. Second, we show explicitly an optimal entry time and an optimal exit time. Meanwhile, a closed-form expression of the maximal expected present value of the project is also obtained.

It is carefully studied that how the jump terms of Lévy processes affect the optimal entry and exit times. We may interpret jumps as information involving both negative and positive influences on the price, and the intensity of jumps as the frequency of information arrivals. By the analysis in Section 3.5, we reach the following conclusions. First, as negative influences increase (or, equivalently, positive influences decrease), the optimal exit time gets earlier. Second, there is a critical point of negative influences above which the behavior of optimal entry times is the same as that of optimal exit times, and below which, however, opposite. Third, if negative influences dominate positive ones, exit times should be scheduled earlier while the frequency of information arrivals becomes higher, and entry times should be scheduled later (earlier) as the frequency increases provided the frequency is below (above) a critical level. Finally, if positive influences dominate negative ones, both the optimal entry time and the optimal exit time increase monotonically with the frequency of information arrivals increasing.

We outline the structure of this chapter. In Section 3.2, we recall how to solve optimal stopping problems through Wiener-Hopf factorization. In Section 3.3, we describe the model in detail. In Section 3.4, we provide explicitly an answer to the problem (see Theorems 3.4.1 and 3.4.11). In Section 3.5, we investigate the effect of jumping of Lévy processes on optimal entry and exit times. Some conclusions are drawn in Section 3.6.

3.2 Solving optimal stopping problems by Wiener-Hopf factorization

In this section, we recall briefly some results of solving optimal stopping problems by Wiener-Hopf factorization. For details, we refer to [6, Chapter 11].

Let X be a Lévy process with Lévy exponent

$$\psi(z) := \mu z + \frac{1}{2}\sigma^2 z^2 + \frac{c^- z}{q^- - z} + \frac{c^+ z}{q^+ - z},$$

where $\mu \in \mathbb{R}$, $\sigma > 0$, $c^{\pm} > 0$ and $q^- < 0 < q^+$.

Set $\overline{X}(t) := \max_{0\leq s\leq t} X(t)$ and $\underline{X}(t) := \min_{0\leq s\leq t} X(t)$. Let T be an exponential random variable on $\mathbb{R}^+$ with mean $1/r$, independent of the process X. Define the operators $\mathcal{E}$, $\mathcal{E}^+$ and $\mathcal{E}^-$ as follows:

$$\mathcal{E}g(x) := \mathbb{E}[g(x + X(T))],$$

$$\mathcal{E}^+g(x) := \mathbb{E}[g(x + \overline{X}(T))]$$

and

$$\mathcal{E}^-g(x) := \mathbb{E}[g(x + \underline{X}(T))].$$

We have Wiener-Hopf factorization $\mathcal{E} = \mathcal{E}^+\mathcal{E}^-$.

To obtain explicit formulas for $\mathcal{E}^{\pm}$, we first express

$$\kappa^+(z) := \mathbb{E}[\exp(z\overline{X}(T))]$$

and

$$\kappa^-(z) := \mathbb{E}[\exp(z\underline{X}(T))]$$

explicitly.

To this end, let $\beta_j^\pm$, $j = 1, 2$, be the solutions to $r - \psi(z) = 0$ with $\beta_2^- < q^- < \beta_1^- < 0 < \beta_1^+ < q^+ < \beta_2^+$. We have

$$\kappa^\pm(z) = \frac{\beta_1^\pm}{\beta_1^\pm - z} \times \frac{\beta_2^\pm}{\beta_2^\pm - z} \times \frac{q^\pm - z}{q^\pm} \tag{3.2.1}$$

and

$$\kappa^\pm(z) = a_1^\pm \frac{\beta_1^\pm}{\beta_1^\pm - z} + a_2^\pm \frac{\beta_2^\pm}{\beta_2^\pm - z},$$

where

$$a_1^\pm = \frac{\beta_2^\pm}{\beta_2^\pm - \beta_1^\pm} \times \frac{q^\pm - \beta_1^\pm}{q^\pm}, \text{ and } a_2^\pm = \frac{\beta_1^\pm}{\beta_1^\pm - \beta_2^\pm} \times \frac{q^\pm - \beta_2^\pm}{q^\pm}.$$

After these preparations, we get the explicit expressions for $\mathcal{E}^\pm$:

$$\mathcal{E}^+ g(x) = \sum_{j=1}^{2} a_j^+ \int_0^{+\infty} \beta_j^+ \exp(-\beta_j^+ y) g(x+y) \mathrm{d}y$$

and

$$\mathcal{E}^- g(x) = \sum_{j=1}^{2} a_j^- \int_{-\infty}^{0} \left(-\beta_j^- \exp(-\beta_j^- y) g(x+y)\right) \mathrm{d}y.$$

The inverses of $\mathcal{E}^\pm$ are given by

$$(\mathcal{E}^+)^{-1} g(x) = -c_+^1 g'(x) + c_+^0 g(x) + \int_0^{+\infty} b_+ q^+ \exp(-q^+ y) g(x+y) \mathrm{d}y$$

and

$$(\mathcal{E}^-)^{-1} g(x) = -c_-^1 g'(x) + c_-^0 g(x) - \int_{-\infty}^{0} b_- q^- \exp(-q^- y) g(x+y) \mathrm{d}y,$$

where

$$c_\pm^1 := \frac{q^\pm}{\beta_1^\pm \beta_2^\pm}, \; c_\pm^0 = (\beta_1^\pm + \beta_2^\pm - q^\pm) c_\pm^1, \text{ and } b_\pm = 1 - c_\pm^0.$$

The following facts

$$\begin{aligned} &\mathcal{E}^\pm 1 = 1, && \mathcal{E}^\pm g(x) = \kappa^\pm(z) g(x), \\ &(\mathcal{E}^\pm)^{-1} 1 = 1, && (\mathcal{E}^\pm)^{-1} g(x) = (\kappa^\pm)^{-1}(z) g(x), \end{aligned}$$

where $g(x) := \exp(zx)$ for $z \in \mathbb{C}$, are frequently used.

We apply the following two theorems in this chapter.

Theorem 3.2.1 (cf. [6, p. 204, Theorem 11.4.2; p. 208, Theorem 11.5.1]) *Assume that*

(A1) $r - \psi(z) > 0$ *for all* $z \in [\sigma^-, \sigma^+]$ *with* $\sigma^- < 0 < \sigma^+$,

(A2) $g(x)$ *is measurable and satisfies the bound* $|g(x)| \le C(\exp(\sigma^- x) + \exp(\sigma^+ x))$ *for some constant* C, *and*

(A3) *there exists* h_* *such that* $\mathcal{E}^+ g(x) < 0$ *for any* $x < h_*$ *and* $\mathcal{E}^+ g(x) > 0$ *for any* $x > h_*$.

Then $\inf\{t : x + X(t) \le h_*\}$ *is a solution of the optimal stopping problem*

$$V(x) := \sup_{\tau \in \mathcal{T}} \mathbb{E}\left[\int_0^\tau \exp(-rt) g(x + X(t)) \mathrm{d}t\right],$$

where $\mathcal{T}$ *is the collection of all stopping times, and*

$$V(x) = r^{-1}(\mathcal{E}^- \mathbf{1}_{(h_*, +\infty)} \mathcal{E}^+ g)(x) \text{ for } x > h_* \quad \text{and} \quad V(x) = 0 \text{ for } x \le h_*.$$

Theorem 3.2.2 (cf. [6, p. 207, Theorem 11.4.7; p. 211, Theorem 11.5.5]) *Assume that*

(A1) $r - \psi(z) > 0$ *for all* $z \in [\sigma^-, \sigma^+]$ *with* $\sigma^- < 0 < \sigma^+$,

(A2) $G(x)$ *is twice differentiable a.e., and for any* N, *there exists constant* C *such that* $\left|\sum_{j=0}^{2} G^{(j)}(x)\right| \le C \exp(\sigma^+ x)$ *on* $(N, +\infty)$ *a.e., and*

(A3) *there exists* h_* *such that* $(\mathcal{E}^+)^{-1} G(x) < 0$ *for any* $x < h_*$ *and* $(\mathcal{E}^+)^{-1} G(x) > 0$ *for any* $x > h_*$.

Then $\inf\{t : x + X(t) \ge h_*\}$ *is a solution of the optimal stopping problem*

$$V(x) := \sup_{\tau \in \mathcal{T}} \mathbb{E}\left[\exp(-r\tau) G(x + X(\tau))\right],$$

where $\mathcal{T}$ *is the collection of all stopping times, and*

$$V(x) = (\mathcal{E}^+ \mathbf{1}_{[h_*, +\infty)} (\mathcal{E}^+)^{-1} G)(x) \text{ for } x < h_* \quad \text{and} \quad V(x) = G(x) \text{ for } x \ge h_*.$$

3.3 The model

Consider a Lévy process X with Lévy-Itô decomposition

$$X(t) = \mu t + \sigma B(t) + \sum_{k=1}^{N(t)} Y_k, \tag{3.3.1}$$

where $\mu \in \mathbb{R}$, $\sigma > 0$, B is a standard Brownian motion, N is a Poission process of intensity λ, and $\{Y_k\}_{k\in\mathbb{N}}$ is a sequence of i.i.d. random variables with a common pdf f given by

$$f(y) := -b_1 q^- \exp(-q^- y)\mathbf{1}_{\{y<0\}} + b_2 q^+ \exp(-q^+ y)\mathbf{1}_{\{y>0\}}$$

for $b_1, b_2 > 0$, $b_1 + b_2 = 1$ and $q^- < 0 < q^+$.

We assume that the price process follows $\exp(x + X(t))$ for some $x \in \mathbb{R}$.

To schedule the project optimally, we will solve the following problem:

$$\begin{aligned} J(x) := \sup_{\tau_I \le \tau_O} \mathbb{E}\Bigg[\int_{\tau_I}^{\tau_O} & \exp(-rt)(\exp(x + X(t)) - C)dt - \\ & \exp(-r\tau_I)K_I - \exp(-r\tau_O)K_O\Bigg], \end{aligned} \tag{3.3.2}$$

where τ_I and τ_O are stopping times, r is the discount rate such that $r > 0$, C is the running cost, K_I is the entry cost, and K_O is the exit cost. We call stopping times τ_I and τ_O entry times and exit times, respectively, and the function J the maximal expected present value of the project. We assume $K_I + K_O \ge 0$ in order to eliminate the arbitrage opportunity which is to enter the project and then immediately exit it.

3.4 An optimal entry-exit decision

In this section, we provide an optimal entry-exit decision and an explicit expression for the function J (see (3.3.2)).

Let us first consider a simple case

$$\mu + \frac{1}{2}\sigma^2 + \lambda(\mathbb{E}[\exp(Y_1)] - 1) \ge r.$$

In this case, noting

- $B(t)$ is independent of $\sum_{k=1}^{N(t)} Y_k$,
- $\mathbb{E}[\exp(\sigma B(t))] = \exp\left(\sigma^2 t/2\right)$, and
- $\mathbb{E}\left[\exp\left(\sum_{k=1}^{N(t)} Y_k\right)\right] = \exp\left(\lambda\left(\mathbb{E}[\exp(Y_1)] - 1\right) t\right)$,

we get

$$\begin{aligned}
&\mathbb{E}\left[\int_0^{+\infty} \exp(-rt)\exp(x + X(t))\mathrm{d}t\right] \\
&= \exp(x)\int_0^{+\infty} \exp\left[\left(\mu + \frac{1}{2}\sigma^2 + \lambda(\mathbb{E}[\exp(Y_1)] - 1) - r\right)t\right]\mathrm{d}t \\
&= +\infty.
\end{aligned}$$

Thus we obtain the following result.

Theorem 3.4.1 *Assume that*

$$\mu + \frac{1}{2}\sigma^2 + \lambda(\mathbb{E}[\exp(Y_1)] - 1) \geq r.$$

Then $\tau_I^* := 0$ a.s. is an optimal entry time and $\tau_O^* := +\infty$ a.s. is an optimal exit time, i.e., the firm should never exit the project. In addition, the function J in (3.3.2) is given by $J \equiv +\infty$.

Corollary 3.4.2 *If $q^+ \leq 1$, the conclusions in Theorem 3.4.1 hold.*

Proof. It follows from $\mathbb{E}[\exp(Y_1)] = +\infty$ iff $q^+ \leq 1$. □

Next, we determine an optimal entry-exit decision for the case

$$\mu + \frac{1}{2}\sigma^2 + \lambda(\mathbb{E}[\exp(Y_1)] - 1) < r. \tag{3.4.1}$$

To this end, we first solve the following two optimal stopping problems:

(3.4.2)

$$G(x) := \sup_{\tau_O} \mathbb{E}\left[\int_0^{\tau_O} \exp(-rt)(\exp(x + X(t)) - C)\mathrm{d}t - \exp(-r\tau_O)K_O\right]$$

and

$$H(x) := \sup_{\tau_I} \mathbb{E}\left[\exp(-r\tau_I)\left(G(x + X(\tau_I)) - K_I\right)\right], \tag{3.4.3}$$

then show an optimal entry-exit decision based on the results of (3.4.2) and (3.4.3).

Noting that

– $B(1)$ is independent of $\sum_{k=1}^{N(1)} Y_k$,

– $\mathbb{E}[\exp(z\sigma B(1))] = \exp\left(\sigma^2 z^2/2\right)$, and

– $\mathbb{E}\left[\exp\left(z\sum_{k=1}^{N(1)} Y_k\right)\right] = \exp\left(\frac{\lambda b^- z}{q^- - z} + \frac{\lambda b^+ z}{q^+ - z}\right)$,

we see that the Lévy exponent ψ of the Lévy process (3.3.1) is given by

$$\psi(z) = \mu z + \frac{1}{2}\sigma^2 z^2 + \frac{\lambda b^- z}{q^- - z} + \frac{\lambda b^+ z}{q^+ - z}.$$

Thus the condition (3.4.1) is equivalent to $\psi(1) < r$.

Lemma 3.4.3 *If $\psi(1) < r$, then*

① *$\kappa^+(1) > 1$;*

② *there exist numbers σ^- and σ^+ with $\sigma^- < 0 < 1 < \sigma^+$ such that $r - \psi(z) > 0$ for all $z \in [\sigma^-, \sigma^+]$.*

Proof. Note that $\psi(1) < r$ implies $q^+, \beta_1^+ > 1$. Then the conclusion ① follows by the expression (3.2.1) of κ^+, and the conclusion ② holds since $r - \psi(z) > 0$ for all $z \in (\beta_1^-, \beta_1^+)$. □

Theorem 3.4.4 *For the optimal stopping problem* (3.4.2), *the following are true.*

① *If $\psi(1) < r$ and $C \le rK_O$, then $\tau_O^* := +\infty$ a.s. is a solution of* (3.4.2). *In addition, $G(x) = \exp(x)/(r - \psi(1)) - C/r$.*

② *If $\psi(1) < r$ and $C > rK_O$, then $\tau_O^* := \inf\{t > 0 : x + X(t) \le h_O\}$ is a solution of* (3.4.2), *where*

$$h_O = \log\left(\frac{C - rK_O}{\kappa^+(1)}\right).$$

In addition,

$$G(x)=\begin{cases}\dfrac{\exp(x)}{r-\psi(1)}-\dfrac{C}{r}+\dfrac{C-rK_O}{r}\displaystyle\sum_{j=1}^{2}\frac{a_j^-}{1-\beta_j^-}\exp(\beta_j^-(x-h_O)) \\ \qquad\qquad\qquad\qquad\qquad\qquad\qquad\qquad \text{if } x>h_O, \\ -K_O \ \text{if } x\le h_O.\end{cases}$$

Proof. (1) Assume that $\psi(1)<r$ and $C\le rK_O$.

Noting that for any $\tau>0$

$$\begin{aligned}&\int_0^\tau \exp(-rt)(\exp(x+X(t))-C)\mathrm{d}t-\exp(-r\tau)K_O\\ =&\int_0^\tau \exp(-rt)(\exp(x+X(t))-C+rK_O)\mathrm{d}t-K_O,\end{aligned}\tag{3.4.4}$$

we find $\tau_O^*:=+\infty$ a.s. is a solution of (3.4.2) and

$$G(x)=\frac{\exp(x)}{r-\psi(1)}-\frac{C}{r}.$$

(2) Assume that $\psi(1)<r$ and $C>rK_O$.

We check whether the conditions (A1)–(A3) in Theorem 3.2.1 are met.

The conclusion ② of Lemma 3.4.3 tells us (A1) holds.

It follows (3.4.4) and $g(x):=\exp(x)-C+rK_O$ that (A2) is satisfied.

By Lemma 3.4.3, define $h_O:=\log[(C-rK_O)/\kappa^+(1)]$. A straight calculation shows that $\mathcal{E}^+g(x)=\kappa^+(1)\exp(x)-C+rK_O$. Thus $\mathcal{E}^+g(x)<0$ for any $x<h_O$ and $\mathcal{E}^+g(x)>0$ for any $x>h_O$, and (A3) follows.

Applying Theorem 3.2.1, we obtain

$$G(x)=\frac{\exp(x)}{r-\psi(1)}-\frac{C}{r}+\frac{C-rK_O}{r}\sum_{j=1}^{2}\frac{a_j^-}{1-\beta_j^-}\exp[\beta_j^-(x-h_O)] \text{ for } x>h_O,$$

and $G(x)=-K_O$ for $x\le h_O$. □

Remark 3.4.5 We will prove in Theorem 3.4.11 that $\exp(h_O)$ is a trigger price of optimal exit times.

Corollary 3.4.6 *The optimal exit trigger price* $\exp(h_O)$ *in Theorem 3.4.4 satisfies* $\exp(h_O)<C-rK_O$.

Proof. Note that $\exp(h_O) = (C - rK_O)/\kappa^+(1)$. Then, thanks to ① of Lemma 3.4.3, the conclusion follows. □

Theorem 3.4.7 *For the optimal stopping problem* (3.4.3), *the following are true.*

① *If* $\psi(1) < r$, $C - rK_O \le 0$ *and* $C + rK_I \le 0$, *then* $\tau_I^* := 0$ *a.s. is a solution of* (3.4.3). *In addition,*

$$H(x) = \frac{\exp(x)}{r - \psi(1)} - \frac{C}{r} - K_I.$$

② *If* $\psi(1) < r$, $C - rK_O \le 0$ *and* $C + rK_I > 0$, *then* $\tau_I^* := \inf\{t : t > 0, x + X(t) \ge h_I\}$ *is a solution of* (3.4.3), *where*

$$h_I = \log\left(\frac{C + rK_I}{\kappa^-(1)}\right).$$

In addition,

$$H(x) = \begin{cases} \dfrac{C + rK_I}{r} \displaystyle\sum_{j=1}^{2} \frac{a_j^+}{\beta_j^+ - 1} \exp[\beta_j^+(x - h_I)], & \text{if } x < h_I, \\ \dfrac{\exp(x)}{r - \psi(1)} - \dfrac{C}{r} - K_I, & \text{if } x \ge h_I. \end{cases}$$

③ *If* $\psi(1) < r$ *and* $C - rK_O > 0$, *then* $\tau_I^* := \inf\{t : t > 0, x + X(t) \ge h_I\}$ *is a solution of* (3.4.3), *where* h_I *is the solution of*

$$\frac{1}{\kappa^+(1)} \frac{\exp(x)}{r - \psi(1)} - \frac{C}{r} - K_I + \frac{C - rK_O}{r} \sum_{j=1}^{2} \frac{a_j^-}{1 - \beta_j^-} \frac{\exp[\beta_j^-(x - h_O)]}{\kappa^+(\beta_j^-)} = 0$$

on $(h_O, +\infty)$.

In addition,

$$H(x) = \frac{\exp(h_I)}{\kappa^+(1)(r - \psi(1))} \sum_{j=1}^{2} \frac{a_j^+ \beta_j^+}{\beta_j^+ - 1} \exp[\beta_j^+(x - h_I)] -$$

$$\frac{C + rK_I}{r} \sum_{j=1}^{2} a_j^+ \exp[\beta_j^+(x - h_I)] +$$

$$\frac{C - rK_O}{r} \sum_{j,k=1}^{2} \frac{a_k^-}{1 - \beta_k^-} \times \frac{a_j^+ \beta_j^+}{\beta_j^+ - \beta_k^-} \times \frac{\exp[\beta_k^-(h_I - h_O)]}{\kappa^+(\beta_k^-)} \exp[\beta_j^+(x - h_I)]$$

for $x < h_I$, *and*

$$H(x) = \frac{\exp(x)}{r-\psi(1)} - \frac{C}{r} - K_I + \frac{C - rK_O}{r}\sum_{j=1}^{2}\frac{a_j^-}{1-\beta_j^-}\exp[\beta_j^-(x-h_O)]$$

for $x \geq h_I$.

Proof. (1) Assume that $\psi(1) < r$, $C - rK_O \leq 0$ and $C + rK_I \leq 0$.

Let τ and k be any stopping time and positive integer, respectively. Define $F(x) := \exp(x)/(r-\psi(1)) - C/r - K_I$ and $\tau_k := \inf\{t : t > 0 \text{ and } |X(t)| > k\} \wedge \tau \wedge k$. By Itô formula, we get

$$\begin{aligned}
&\exp(-r\tau_k)F(x+X(\tau_k)) \\
&= F(x) + \int_0^{\tau_k}\exp(-rt)(\mathcal{L}-r)F(x+X(t))\mathrm{d}t + \\
&\quad \text{the time } \tau_k \text{ value of a martingale vanishing at time zero} \\
&= F(x) + \int_0^{\tau_k}[-\exp(x+X(t)) + C + rK_I]\mathrm{d}t + \\
&\quad \text{the time } \tau_k \text{ value of a martingale vanishing at time zero,}
\end{aligned} \tag{3.4.5}$$

where $\mathcal{L}$ is the infinitesimal generator of X.

Taking expectations in (3.4.5), and noting $C + rK_I \leq 0$, we have

$$\mathbb{E}\left[\exp(-r\tau_k)F(x+X(\tau_k))\right] \leq F(x),$$

i.e.,

$$\mathbb{E}\left[\exp(-r\tau_k)\left(\frac{\exp(x+X(\tau_k))}{r-\psi(1)} - \frac{C}{r} - K_I\right)\right] \leq \frac{\exp(x)}{r-\psi(1)} - \frac{C}{r} - K_I.$$

Sending $k \to +\infty$ in the above inequality and applying Fatou's lemma, we find

$$\mathbb{E}\left[\exp(-r\tau)\left(\frac{\exp(x+X(\tau))}{r-\psi(1)} - \frac{C}{r} - K_I\right)\right] \leq \frac{\exp(x)}{r-\psi(1)} - \frac{C}{r} - K_I,$$

which proves ①.

(2) Assume that $\psi(1) < r$, $C - rK_O \leq 0$ and $C + rK_I > 0$.

Here, we only need to verify (A3) in Theorem 3.2.2 as the examination of (A1) and (A2) is similar to the related content of the proof of Theorem 3.4.4.

Some straight calculations show us that

$$(\mathcal{E}^+)^{-1}(G-K_I)(x)=\frac{1}{\kappa^+(1)}\frac{\exp(x)}{r-\psi(1)}-\frac{C}{r}-K_I \quad \text{for any } x\in\mathbb{R}.$$

Set

$$\begin{aligned} h_I:&=\log\left[\kappa^+(1)\times(r-\psi(1))\times\frac{C+rK_I}{r}\right]\\ &=\log\left(\frac{C+rK_I}{\kappa^-(1)}\right). \end{aligned}$$

It follows that

$$(\mathcal{E}^+)^{-1}(G-K_I)(x)<0 \text{ for } x<h_I \text{ and } (\mathcal{E}^+)^{-1}(G-K_I)(x)>0 \text{ for } x>h_I.$$

Then by Theorem 3.2.2 we get, for $x<h_I$,

$$\begin{aligned} H(x)&=\mathcal{E}^+\mathbf{1}_{[h_I,+\infty)}(\mathcal{E}^+)^{-1}(G-K_I)(x)\\ &=\frac{\exp(h_I)}{\kappa^+(1)(r-\psi(1))}\sum_{j=1}^{2}\frac{a_j^+\beta_j^+}{\beta_j^+-1}\exp[\beta_j^+(x-h_I)]-\\ &\quad\frac{C+rK_I}{r}\sum_{j=1}^{2}a_j^+\exp[\beta_j^+(x-h_I)]\\ &=\frac{C+rK_I}{r}\sum_{j=1}^{2}\frac{a_j^+}{\beta_j^+-1}\exp[\beta_j^+(x-h_I)]. \end{aligned}$$

(3) Assume that $\psi(1)<r$ and $C-rK_O\geq 0$.

By the same reason as Step 2, we only need to check (A3). The expression of $(\mathcal{E}^+)^{-1}(G-K_I)$ is as follows.

$$\begin{aligned} (\mathcal{E}^+)^{-1}(G-K_I)(x)=&\frac{1}{\kappa^+(1)}\frac{\exp(x)}{r-\psi(1)}-\frac{C}{r}-K_I+\\ &\frac{C-rK_O}{r}\sum_{j=1}^{2}\frac{a_j^-}{1-\beta_j^-}\frac{\exp[\beta_j^-(x-h_O)]}{\kappa^+(\beta_j^-)} \end{aligned}$$

for $x>h_O$, and

$$(\mathcal{E}^+)^{-1}(G-K_I)(x)=-K_I-K_O-b_+\sum_{j=1}^{2}\frac{a_j^-\beta_j^-\exp[q^+(x-h_O)]}{(q^+-1)(q^+-\beta_j^-)} \quad \text{for } x\leq h_O.$$

Noting that $b_+ < 0$, $a_j^- > 0$, $\beta_j^- < 0$, $q^+ > 1$ and $K_I + K_O \geq 0$, we find that

$$(\mathcal{E}^+)^{-1}(G - K_I)(x) < 0 \quad \text{for } x \leq h_O.$$

Together with $\lim_{x \to +\infty} (\mathcal{E}^+)^{-1}(G - K_I)(x) = +\infty$ and the convexity of $(\mathcal{E}^+)^{-1}(G - K_I)(\cdot)$ on $(h_O, +\infty)$, we then see that $(\mathcal{E}^+)^{-1}(G - K_I)(\cdot)$ has only one zero point, say, h_I, such that $(\mathcal{E}^+)^{-1}(G - K_I)(x)$ for $x < h_I$ and $(\mathcal{E}^+)^{-1}(G - K_I)(x)$ for $x > h_I$.

Applying Theorem 3.2.2 we have, for $x < h_I$,

$$H(x) = \frac{\exp(h_I)}{\kappa^+(1)(r - \psi(1))} \sum_{j=1}^{2} \frac{a_j^+ \beta_j^+}{\beta_j^+ - 1} \exp[\beta_j^+(x - h_I)] -$$

$$\frac{C + rK_I}{r} \sum_{j=1}^{2} a_j^+ \exp[\beta_j^+(x - h_I)] +$$

$$\frac{C - rK_O}{r} \sum_{j,k=1}^{2} \frac{a_k^-}{1 - \beta_k^-} \frac{a_j^+ \beta_j^+}{\beta_j^+ - \beta_k^-} \frac{\exp[\beta_k^-(h_I - h_O)]}{\kappa^+(\beta_k^-)} \exp[\beta_j^+(x - h_I)],$$

and ③ follows. □

Remark 3.4.8 Theorem 3.4.11 shows that such prices $\exp(h_I)$ are trigger prices of optimal entry times.

Corollary 3.4.9 *The optimal exit trigger prices* $\exp(h_I)$ *in Theorem 3.4.7 satisfy* $\exp(h_I) > C + rK_I$.

To prove Corollary 3.4.9 we need the following proposition concerning G and H.

Proposition 3.4.10 *Let $\mathcal{L}$ be the infinitesimal generator of X. Then the following hold.*

① *G is a viscosity solution of*

$$\min\{ru - \mathcal{L}u - \exp(\cdot) + C, u + K_O\} = 0 \quad \text{on } \mathbb{R}.$$

In particular,

$$rG(h_I) - \mathcal{L}G(h_I) = \exp(h_I) - C.$$

② *H is a viscosity solution of*

$$\min\{ru - \mathcal{L}u, u - G + K_I\} = 0 \quad \text{on } \mathbb{R}.$$

In particular, $H(h_I) = G(h_I) - K_I$, *and* $H(x) \geq G(x) - K_I$ *for all* $x \in \mathbb{R}$.

Proof. The conclusions follow from the classical optimal stopping theory (see, e.g., [35, p. 137, Theorem 9.2]). □

Proof of Corollary 3.4.9. (1) Assume that $\psi(1) < r$, $C - rK_O \leq 0$ and $C + rK_I > 0$.

Noting that $\kappa^-(1) < 1$ by expression (3.2.1) of κ^-, we get $\exp(h_I) > C + rK_I$ since $h_I = \log[(C + rK_I)/\kappa^-(1)]$.

(2) Assume that $\psi(1) < r$ and $C - rK_O \geq 0$.

We first prove $H''_-(h_I) \geq G''(h_I)$ by contradiction. Suppose that $H''_-(h_I) < G''(h_I)$. Then there exists a positive number δ such that $H''(x) < G''(x)$ for all $x \in (h_I - \delta, h_I)$. Consequently, together with $H'(h_I) = G'(h_I)$, it follows that $H'(x) > G'(x)$ for all $x \in (h_I - \delta, h_I)$, and then, as $H(h_I) = G(h_I) - K_I$, $H(x) < G(x) - K_I$ for all $x \in (h_I - \delta, h_I)$, which contradicts $H(x) \geq G(x) - K_I$ for all $x \in \mathbb{R}$.

It follows $H''_-(h_I) \geq G''(h_I)$ and Proposition 3.4.10 that

$$r(G(h_I) - K_I) - \mu G'(h_I) - \frac{1}{2}\sigma^2 G''(h_I) - \int_{\mathbb{R}} (G(h_I + y) - G(h_I))\nu(\mathrm{d}y)$$

$$> rH(h_I) - \mu H'(h_I) - \frac{1}{2}\sigma^2 H''_-(h_I) - \int_{\mathbb{R}} (H(h_I + y) - H(h_I))\nu(\mathrm{d}y),$$

where ν is the Lévy measure associated with X, i.e., $\exp(h_I) > C + rK_I$ also by Proposition 3.4.10. □

The following Theorem 3.4.11 provides a solution to optimal entry and exit times and an explicit expression of the maximal expected present value of the project.

Theorem 3.4.11 *In each case of Theorem 3.4.7,* τ_I^* *is an optimal entry time, and* τ_O^* *is an optimal exit time, where* $\tau_O^* := +\infty$ *a.s. if* $C \leq rK_O$ *and* $\tau_O^* := \inf\{t : t > \tau_I^* \text{ and } x + X(t) \leq h_O\}$ *if* $C > rK_O$, *respectively. In addition, we have* $J(p) = H(p)$.

Proof. The proof is similar to that of Theorem 1.5.10, but using Proposition 3.4.10 and Lemma 3.4.12. □

Lemma 3.4.12 *Assume that* $\psi(1) < r$. *Then the family of random variables* $\left\{\exp\left[(\mu - r)\tau + \sigma B(\tau) + \sum_{k=1}^{N(\tau)} Y_k\right] : \tau \in \mathcal{T}\right\}$ *is uniformly integrable, where* $\mathcal{T}$ *is the collection of all stopping times.*

Proof. The proof is similar to that of Lemma 1.4.1.

Define $Z(t) := \exp\left[(\mu - r)t + \sigma B(t) + \sum_{k=1}^{N(t)} Y_k\right]$ for any $t \geq 0$. Taking a real number $\alpha > 1$ such that $\psi(\alpha) < \alpha r$ as $\psi(1) < r$, we have for any $s \leq t$

$$\mathbb{E}\left[Z(t)^\alpha | \mathscr{F}_s\right] = \exp[(\psi(\alpha) - \alpha r)(t - s)]Z(s)^\alpha \leq Z(s)^\alpha,$$

which implies that $(Z(t)^\alpha, t \geq 0)$ is a supermartingale with a last element 0. Here, $\mathscr{F}$ is the augmentation of the natural filtration generated by X.

Thus by Doob's optional sampling theorem (see [28, p. 19, Theorem 3.22] or [38, p. 9, Theorem 16]), we get

$$\mathbb{E}\left[X(\tau)^\alpha\right] \leq X(0)^\alpha = 1,$$

for any stopping time τ, and then the lemma follows according to [38, pp. 8–9, Theorem 11]. □

3.5 The effect of jumping on optimal entry-exit decisions

We study by numerical analysis the effect of jumping of X on optimal entry-exit decisions. Recall the form (3.3.1) of X:

$$X(t) = \mu t + \sigma B(t) + \sum_{k=1}^{N(t)} Y_k,$$

where the pdf f of Y_k is

$$f(y) := -b_1 q^- \exp(-q^- y)\mathbf{1}_{\{y<0\}} + b_2 q^+ \exp(-q^+ y)\mathbf{1}_{\{y>0\}}.$$

We can regard each Y_k as news, information, policy, etc., which possesses a *negative* side and a *positive* side. The negative one is indicated by

$-b_1q^- \exp(-q^-y)\mathbf{1}_{\{y<0\}}$, and the positive one $b_2q^+ \exp(-q^+y)\mathbf{1}_{\{y>0\}}$. The intensity λ of N may be interpreted as the frequency of news arrivals.

We fix some parameters: $\mu = 0.1$, $\sigma = 0.01$, $r = 0.2$, $C = 10$, $K_I = -10$, $K_O = 10$.

(1) λ-h_I and λ-h_O pictures ($q^- = -10$, $q^+ = 10$)

Put $b^- = 0.9$ and $b^+ = 0.1$. From Figure 3.1, we find that if a new policy causes the price decreasing by probability 0.9 (here, we neglect the impact of the drift and diffusion on the price), the optimal exit trigger price is monotonically increasing w.r.t. the frequency of making new policies, which is contrary to the case $b^- = 0.1$ and $b^+ = 0.9$ (see Figure 3.2). Thus the higher the frequency of making bad (good) policies is, the earlier (later) the optimal exit time is.

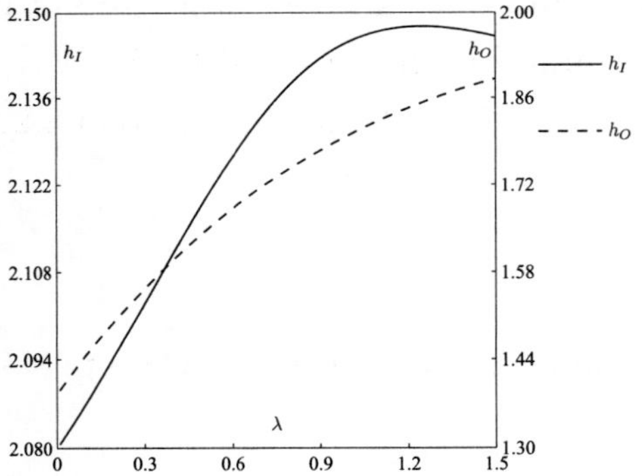

Figure 3.1 λ-h_I (h_O) picture with 90% negative component and 10% positive component

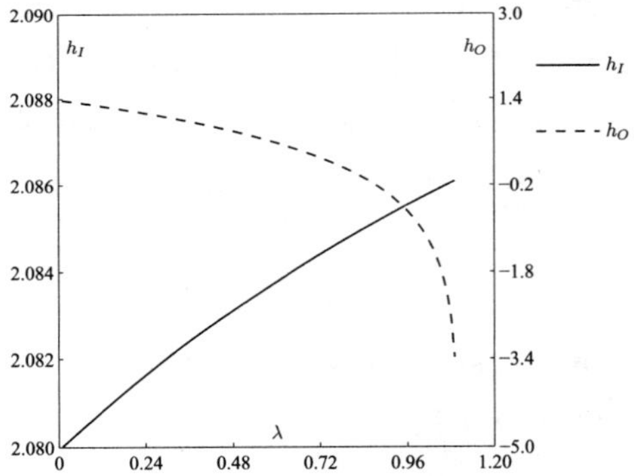

Figure 3.2 λ-h_I (h_O) picture with 10% negative component and 90% positive component

Higher frequencies speed up entries in the bad case but put off entries in the good one, and lower frequencies speed up entries in the both.

(2) q^--h_I and q^--h_O pictures ($q^+ = 10$, $\lambda = 1$)

As running environment becomes worse and worse (since $|q^-|$ is decreasing), the optimal exit time gets an earlier one (since h_O is increasing).

For the optimal entry time, it is a decreasing function in q^- in the bad case (Figure 3.3), but slightly complicated in the good case (Figure 3.4): it is increasing w.r.t. the left q^- and decreasing w.r.t. the right q^-.

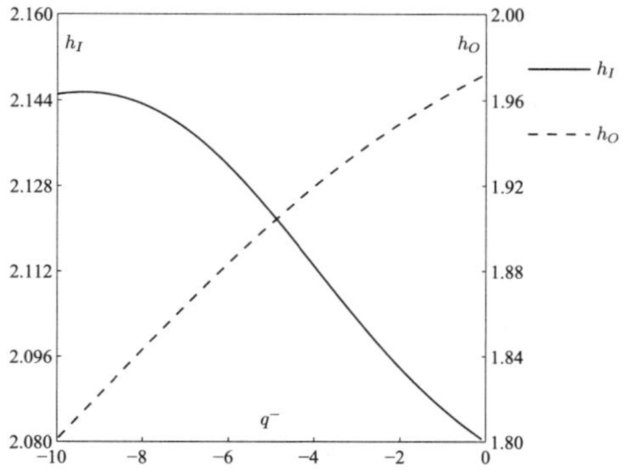

Figure 3.3 q^--h_I (h_O) picture with 90% negative component and 10% positive component

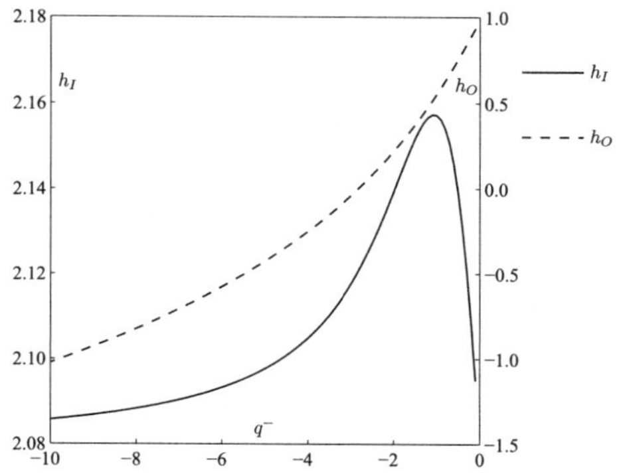

Figure 3.4 q^--h_I (h_O) picture with 10% negative component and 90% positive component

The economic meaning behind Figure 3.4 may be that below a critical point, the positive component prevails, and above this point, the negative component prevails. This tells us that provided the negative influence of news (information, policy, etc.) does not exceed a critical point, investors still have exciting anticipation.

(3) q^+-h_I and q^+-h_O pictures ($q^- = -10$, $\lambda = 1$)

As the positive influence declines, the optimal exit time gets earlier. However, the optimal entry time shows different behaviors in Figure 3.5 and Figure 3.6: in the former, it gets earlier, and in the latter, later.

(4) b^--h_I and b^--h_O pictures ($q^- = -10$, $q^+ = 10$, $\lambda = 1$)

Figure 3.7 is similar to Figure 3.4 except for the convexity of h_O. The picture b^--h_I again tells us that people still have a good forecast as long as the negative influence of information does not exceed a critical point.

3.6 Conclusions

Entry-exit decisions, which appear in various fields, engage many authors. Models of entry-exit decisions were studied under the assumption that price processes follow Itô diffusions, especially, geometric Brownian motions. In practice, some price processes involve jumps. Geometric Lévy processes are

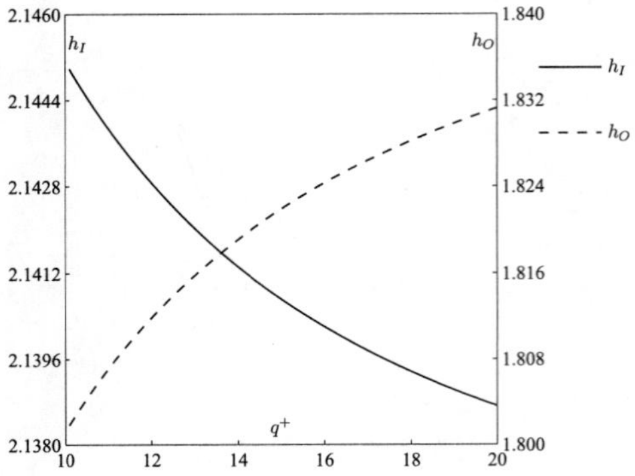

Figure 3.5 q^+-h_I (h_O) picture with 90% negative component and 10% positive component

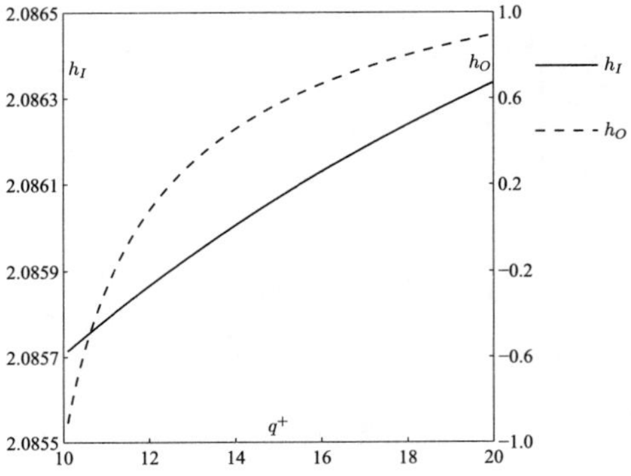

Figure 3.6 q^+-h_I (h_O) picture with 10% negative component and 90% positive component

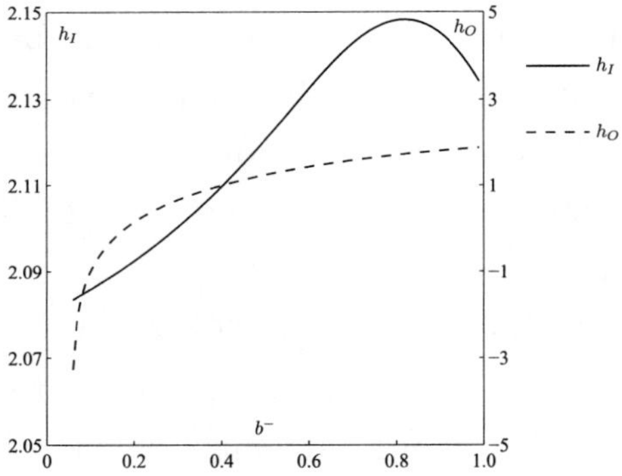

Figure 3.7 b^--h_I (h_O) picture

appropriate candidates for describing such price processes[11, 14, 33]. In this chapter, we study entry-exit decision problems in the context that the log-price process obeys a Lévy process with exponential jumps. We obtain an explicit solution to these problems (see Theorems 3.4.1 and 3.4.11), and discuss intensively the effect of jumping on entry-exit decisions in Section 3.5. The results of the chapter may offer useful materials to investors and policy-makers.

4
Optimal stopping problems with regime switching: a viscosity solution method

Summary: We employ the viscosity solution technique to analyze optimal stopping problems with regime switching. Specifically, we obtain the viscosity property of value functions, uniqueness of viscosity solutions, regularity of value functions and forms of optimal stopping intervals. Finally, we provide an application of the results and achieve closed-form solutions. A numerical example of the application shows that one may put stopping decisions into account within finite time horizon even though he should never give a thought to in some regimes.

4.1 Introduction

Regime-switching processes are appropriate candidates for describing the price of financial assets[2, 12] and the price of some commodities[10]. In addition, as Elias *et al.*[21] pointed out, regime-switching processes are also plausible choices of modeling the stochastic behavior of temperature. Last but not least, regime-switching processes appear in real option pricing[4]. Thus it is reasonable to consider the optimal stopping problems in which underlying processes and payoff functions are modulated by Markov chains.

Many specific problems of optimal stopping with regime switching have been studied. Assuming that the stock price follows a geometric Brownian motion modulated by a two-state Markov chain, Guo[25] provided an explicit closed solution for Russian options. Under the same assumption as that of [25], Guo and Zhang derived an explicit closed solution for perpetual American options in [44] and for optimal selling rules in [24], respectively, and Buffington and Elliot[9] explored American options with finite maturity date. Eloe *et al.*[22] developed optimal selling rules via using a regime-switching exponential Gaussian diffusion model. In a regime-switching Lévy model, Boyarchenko and Levendorskiĭ[5] showed a pricing procedure for perpetual American and real options which is efficient even though the number of states is large provided transition rates are not large with respect to riskless rates. D'Auria and Kella studied in [17] Markov modulation of a two-sided reflected Brownian motion and give an application to fluid queues.

The method used in [e.g., 24, 25, 44] is to construct a solution to some equations by guessing a priori a strategy and then validate it by a verification argument. In this chapter, we will apply the viscosity solution technique to determine solutions of optimal stopping problems with regime switching. First, we prove the value function is a viscosity solution to some variational inequalities. Second, we prove the uniqueness of viscosity solutions. Third, we show the regularity of the value function. Finally, we identify optimal stopping intervals.

We outline the structure of this chapter. In Section 4.2, we prove the viscosity property of the value function of optimal stopping problems with regime switching (Theorem 4.2.2), uniqueness of viscosity solutions (Theorem 4.2.7), regularity of the value function (Theorem 4.2.9) and forms of optimal stopping intervals (Theorem 4.2.13). In Section 4.3, we provide an application of the results obtained in Section 4.2. Some conclusions are drawn in Section 4.4.

4.2 Optimal stopping problems with regime switching

Let $(\Omega, \mathscr{F}, \{\mathscr{F}_t\}_{t\geq 0}, \mathbb{P})$ be a filtered probability space with the filtration $\{\mathscr{F}_t\}_{t\geq 0}$ satisfying the usual conditions and $\mathscr{F}_0$ being the completion of $\{\emptyset, \Omega\}$.

Let $X := (X(t), t \geq 0)$ be a time homogeneous Markov chain defined on $(\Omega, \mathscr{F}, \{\mathscr{F}_t\}_{t\geq 0}, \mathbb{P})$ taking values in the standard orthogonal basis of $\mathbb{R}^m$, $I := \{e_1, e_2, \ldots, e_m\}$, whose rate matrix is $A := (a_{ij})_{m\times m}$ with $a_{ii} < 0$ for each $i = 1, 2, \cdots, m$. Then as in [8], we can show that

$$X(t) = X_0 + \int_0^t AX(s)\mathrm{d}s + M(t),$$

where $M := (M(t), t \geq 0)$ is a martingale with respect to the filtration generated by X.

Let $B := (B(t), t \geq 0)$ be a one dimensional standard Brownian motion, which is independent of X, defined on $(\Omega, \mathscr{F}, \{\mathscr{F}_t\}_{t\geq 0}, \mathbb{P})$.

Assume that the process $Y := (Y(t), t \geq 0)$ satisfies

$$\mathrm{d}Y(t) = \alpha(X(t), Y(t))\mathrm{d}t + \beta(X(t), Y(t))\mathrm{d}B(t), \quad X(0) = e_i, \quad Y(0) = y,$$

where $\alpha : I \times \mathbb{R} \to \mathbb{R}$ and $\beta : I \times \mathbb{R} \to \mathbb{R}$ are two functions such that $\alpha(e_i, \cdot)$ and $\beta(e_i, \cdot)$ are Lipschitz continuous for each $i = 1, 2, \cdots, m$. We assume that $\beta(\cdot, \cdot) > 0$.

Let $\mathcal{T}$ denote the set of all stopping times. For any $\tau \in \mathcal{T}$, $e_i \in I$ and $y \in \mathbb{R}$, we define

$$J^\tau(e_i, y) := \mathbb{E}\Bigg[\int_0^\tau \exp(-rt) f(X(t), Y(t))\mathrm{d}t + \\ \exp(-r\tau) g(X(\tau), Y(\tau)) |\, X(0) = e_i, Y(0) = y\Bigg],$$

where r is a real number, and $f : I \times \mathbb{R} \to \mathbb{R}$ and $g : I \times \mathbb{R} \to \mathbb{R}$ are two functions such that $f(e_i, \cdot)$ and $g(e_i, \cdot)$ are Lipschitz continuous for each $i = 1, 2, \cdots, m$. We assume that $\exp(-r\tau) g(X(\tau), Y(\tau)) = 0$ on $\{\tau = +\infty\}$.

Then the optimal stopping problem with regime switching is described as follows.

(4.2.1)

Find $V(e_i, y)$ and $\tau^* \in \mathcal{T}$ such that $V(e_i, y) = \sup_{\tau \in \mathcal{T}} J^\tau(e_i, y) = J^{\tau^*}(e_i, y)$.

Remark 4.2.1 In literature, people considered the case where the underlying process Y takes a regime-switching geometric Brownian motion such as (4.3.1), $f \equiv 0$, and $g(y) = (K - y)^+$ for American put options or $g(y) = (y - K)$ for selling rules, where K is constant. In the present chapter, we discuss general stopping problems like (4.2.1).

For each $i = 1, 2, \cdots, m$, setting $\alpha_i(\cdot) := \alpha(e_i, \cdot)$, $\beta_i(\cdot) := \beta(e_i, \cdot)$, $f_i(\cdot) := f(e_i, \cdot)$, $g_i(\cdot) := g(e_i, \cdot)$ and $V_i(\cdot) := V(e_i, \cdot)$, we have the following theorem.

Theorem 4.2.2 *Assume that r is large enough. Then for each fixed $i \in \{1, 2, \cdots, m\}$, V_i is the unique viscosity solution with at most linear growth of the variational inequality*

$$\min\left\{rV_i - \mathcal{L}_i V_i - \sum_{q=1}^{m} a_{qi} V_q - f_i, V_i - g_i\right\} = 0 \text{ on } \mathbb{R}, \tag{4.2.2}$$

where $\mathcal{L}$ is defined by

$$\mathcal{L}_i \xi(y) := \frac{1}{2}\beta_i(y)^2 \frac{\partial^2 \xi(y)}{\partial y^2} + \alpha_i(y)\frac{\partial \xi(y)}{\partial y},$$

for any $\xi \in C^2(\mathbb{R})$.

Remark 4.2.3 (1) The assumption that r *is large enough* is nothing but to guarantee the Lipschitz continuity of the functions V_i's. Refer to Lemmas 4.2.5 and 4.3.6.

(2) The uniqueness stated here differs from that in Theorem 4.2.7. Here, for each *fixed* i and V_j, $j = 1, 2, \cdots, i-1, i+1, m$, V_i is the unique viscosity solution to the variational inequality (4.2.2). That is, given the same V_j, $j = 1, 2, \cdots, i-1, i+1, m$, if v is another viscosity solution to the variational inequality (4.2.2), then we get $v = V_i$. However, in Theorem 4.2.7, the uniqueness refers to the uniqueness of a collection of functions. To be specific, if $\{U_1\}_{i=1}^m$ is another collection of functions that fulfills the same condition as $\{V_i\}_{i=1}^m$'s that is stated in Theorem 4.2.2, then we must have $U_i = V_i$ for *all* $i = 1, 2, \cdots, m$.

(3) The uniqueness in Theorem 4.2.2 will be used to prove the regularity of the value function. Refer to Theorem 4.2.9. The uniqueness in Theorem 4.2.7 can determine the value function.

Before proving the above theorem, let us first recall the definition of viscosity solutions.

The theory of viscosity solutions applies to certain partial differential equations of the form $F(x, u, Du, D^2u) = 0$ where $F : \mathbb{R}^N \times \mathbb{R} \times \mathbb{R}^N \times \mathcal{S}(N) \to \mathbb{R}$ along with $\mathcal{S}(N)$ is the set of all symmetric $N \times N$ matrices.

We require F to satisfy the monotonicity condition

$$F(x, r, p, X) \leq F(x, s, p, Y), \text{ whenever } r \leq s \text{ and } Y \leq X. \tag{4.2.3}$$

Here, $r, s \in \mathbb{R}$, $x, p \in \mathbb{R}^N$, $X, Y \in \mathcal{S}(N)$ and $\mathcal{S}(N)$ is equipped with its usual order.

It will be convenient to have the following notations:

$$\mathrm{USC}(\mathcal{O}) := \{\text{upper semicontinuous functions } u : \mathcal{O} \to \mathbb{R}\},$$
$$\mathrm{LSC}(\mathcal{O}) := \{\text{lower semicontinuous functions } u : \mathcal{O} \to \mathbb{R}\},$$

$$J_{\mathcal{O}}^{2,+}u(x) := \{(D\varphi(x), D^2\varphi(x)) : \varphi \text{ is } C^2 \text{ and } u - \varphi \text{ has a maximum at } x\},$$
$$J_{\mathcal{O}}^{2,-}u(x) := \{(D\varphi(x), D^2\varphi(x)) : \varphi \text{ is } C^2 \text{ and } u - \varphi \text{ has a minimum at } x\},$$
$$\overline{J}_{\mathcal{O}}^{2,+}u(x) := \{(p, X) \in \mathbb{R}^N \times \mathcal{S}(N) : \text{there is a sequence } (x_n, p_n, X_n)_{n\in\mathbb{N}} \subset \mathcal{O} \times J_{\mathcal{O}}^{2,+}u(x_n) \text{ such that } (x_n, u(x_n), p_n, X_n) \text{ converges to } (x, u(x), p, X) \text{ as } n \to \infty\},$$
$$\overline{J}_{\mathcal{O}}^{2,-}u(x) := \{(p, X) \in \mathbb{R}^N \times \mathcal{S}(N) : \text{there is a sequence } (x_n, p_n, X_n)_{n\in\mathbb{N}} \subset \mathcal{O} \times J_{\mathcal{O}}^{2,-}u(x_n) \text{ such that } (x_n, u(x_n), p_n, X_n) \text{ converges to } (x, u(x), p, X) \text{ as } n \to \infty\}.$$

Definition 4.2.4 (cf. [16, Definition 2.2]) Let F satisfy (4.2.3) and $\mathcal{O} \subset \mathbb{R}^N$. A viscosity subsolution of $F = 0$ (equivalently, a viscosity solution of $F \leq 0$) on $\mathcal{O}$ is a function $u \in \mathrm{USC}(\mathcal{O})$ such that

$$F(x, u(x), p, X) \leq 0, \text{ for all } x \in \mathcal{O} \text{ and } (p, X) \in J_{\mathcal{O}}^{2,+}u(x).$$

Similarly, a viscosity supersolution of $F = 0$ (equivalently, a viscosity solution of $F \geq 0$) on $\mathcal{O}$ is a function $u \in \mathrm{LSC}(\mathcal{O})$ such that

$$F(x, u(x), p, X) \geq 0, \text{ for all } x \in \mathcal{O} \text{ and } (p, X) \in J_{\mathcal{O}}^{2,-}u(x).$$

Finally, u is a viscosity of $F = 0$ on $\mathcal{O}$ if it is both a viscosity subsolution and a viscosity supersolution of $F = 0$ on $\mathcal{O}$.

The following lemma is used in the proof of Theorem 4.2.2.

Lemma 4.2.5 *There is a positive number r_0 such that V_i is Lipschitz continuous for each $i = 1, 2, \cdots, m$ if $r > r_0$.*

Proof. The proof is similar to that of [36, p. 96, Lemma 5.2.1]. □

Now we provide a proof of Theorem 4.2.2.

Proof of Theorem 4.2.2. (1) Following [42, Section 4.2], we have the dynamic programming principle (4.2.4). Also refer to [20, Theorem 4]. For any $j \in \{1, 2, \cdots, m\}$, $y \in \mathbb{R}$ and $\theta \in \mathcal{T}$, we have

$$\begin{aligned} V_j(y) = \sup_{\tau\in\mathcal{T}} \mathbb{E}\bigg[\int_0^{\theta\wedge\tau} & \exp(-rt)f(X(t), Y(t))\mathrm{d}t + \\ & \exp(-r\tau)g(X(\tau), Y(\tau))\mathbf{1}_{\{\theta>\tau\}} + \\ & \exp(-r\theta)V(X(\theta), Y(\theta))\mathbf{1}_{\{\theta\le\tau\}}\Big|X(0) = e_j, Y(0) = y\bigg]. \end{aligned} \tag{4.2.4}$$

(2) *The viscosity supersolution property.* Fix an $i \in \{1, 2, \cdots, m\}$. Suppose that $\varphi_i \in C^2(\mathbb{R})$ and $V_i - \varphi_i$ has a minimum at some point $y_i \in \mathbb{R}$ such that $V_i(y_i) = \varphi_i(y_i)$. For any positive integer k, choose some functions $\varphi_j^k \in C^2(\mathbb{R})$ such that $\max_{y\in\mathbb{R}} |\varphi_j^k(y) - V_j(y)| < 1/k$, where $j \neq i$ (see, for example, [50, p. 63, Lemma 1.3]). Set $\varphi_i^k := \varphi_i$ for convenience.

Define a stopping time $\theta_0 := \inf\{t : t > 0, (X(t), Y(t)) \notin \{e_i\} \times (y_i - 1, y_i + 1)\}$. Then by the dynamic programming principle (4.2.4), for any positive number ε, we have, via taking $\tau = \theta = \theta_0 \wedge \varepsilon$,

(4.2.5)

$$\begin{aligned} V_i(y_i) \ge \mathbb{E}\bigg[\int_0^{\theta_0\wedge\varepsilon} & \exp(-rt)f(X(t), Y(t))\mathrm{d}t + \\ & \exp[-r(\theta_0\wedge\varepsilon)]V(X(\theta_0\wedge\varepsilon), Y(\theta_0\wedge\varepsilon))\Big|X(0) = e_i, Y(0) = y_i\bigg] \\ \ge -\frac{1}{k} + \mathbb{E}\bigg[\int_0^{\theta_0\wedge\varepsilon} & \exp(-rt)f(X(t), Y(t))\mathrm{d}t + \\ & \exp[-r(\theta_0\wedge\varepsilon)]\sum_{j=1}^m \varphi_j^k(Y(\theta_0\wedge\varepsilon))X_j(\theta_0\wedge\varepsilon)\Big|X(0) = e_i, Y(0) = y_i\bigg]. \end{aligned}$$

In addition, by Itô's formula, we have

(4.2.6)

$$\exp[-r(\theta_0 \wedge \varepsilon)] \sum_{j=1}^{m} \varphi_j^k(Y(\theta_0 \wedge \varepsilon)) X_j(\theta_0 \wedge \varepsilon)$$

$$= \sum_{j=1}^{m} \varphi_j^k(Y(0)) X_j(0) + \sum_{j=1}^{m} \int_0^{\theta_0 \wedge \varepsilon} \exp(-rt) \bigg(\frac{1}{2} \beta(X(t), Y(t))^2 \frac{\partial^2 \varphi_j^k}{\partial y^2}(Y(t)) +$$

$$\alpha(X(t), Y(t)) \frac{\partial \varphi_j^k}{\partial y}(Y(t)) - r\varphi_j^k(Y(t)) + \sum_{q=1}^{m} a_{qj} \varphi_q^k(Y(t)) \bigg) X_j(t) \mathrm{d}t +$$

$$\sum_{j=1}^{m} \int_0^{\theta_0 \wedge \varepsilon} \exp(-rt) \beta(X(t), Y(t)) \frac{\partial \varphi_j^k}{\partial y}(Y(t)) X_j(t) \mathrm{d}B(t) +$$

$$\sum_{j=1}^{m} \int_0^{\theta_0 \wedge \varepsilon} \exp(-rt) \varphi_j^k(Y(t)) \mathrm{d}M_j(t).$$

By combining (4.2.5) and (4.2.6), it follows that

$$\sum_{j=1}^{m} \mathbb{E}\bigg[\frac{1}{\varepsilon} \int_0^{\theta_0 \wedge \varepsilon} \exp(-rt) \bigg(- f_j(Y(t)) + r\varphi_j^k(Y(t)) -$$

$$\frac{1}{2} \beta(X(t), Y(t))^2 \frac{\partial^2 \varphi_j^k}{\partial y^2}(Y(t)) - \alpha(X(t), Y(t)) \frac{\partial \varphi_j^k}{\partial y}(Y(t)) -$$

$$\sum_{q=1}^{m} a_{qj} \varphi_q^k(Y(t)) \bigg) X_j(t) \mathrm{d}t \bigg| X(0) = e_i, Y(0) = y_i \bigg] \geq -\frac{1}{k\varepsilon},$$

i.e., as $X(t) = e_i$ for $t \in (0, \theta_0)$,

$$\mathbb{E}\bigg[\frac{1}{\varepsilon} \int_0^{\theta_0 \wedge \varepsilon} \exp(-rt) \bigg(- f_i(Y(t)) + r\varphi_i(Y(t)) - \mathcal{L}_i \varphi_i(Y(t)) -$$

$$\sum_{q=1}^{m} a_{qi} \varphi_q^k(Y(t)) \bigg) \mathrm{d}t \bigg| X(0) = e_i, Y(0) = y_i \bigg] \geq -\frac{1}{k\varepsilon}.$$

By sending $k \to +\infty$, it follows that

$$\mathbb{E}\bigg[\frac{1}{\varepsilon} \int_0^{\theta_0 \wedge \varepsilon} \exp(-rt) \bigg(- f_i(Y(t)) + r\varphi_i(Y(t)) - \mathcal{L}_i \varphi_i(Y(t)) -$$

$$\sum_{q=1}^{m} a_{qi} V_q(Y(t)) \bigg) \mathrm{d}t \bigg| X(0) = e_i, Y(0) = y_i \bigg] \geq 0.$$

Now taking limits in the above inequality as $\varepsilon \to 0^+$ and applying the mean value theorem, we obtain

$$rV_i(y_i) - \mathcal{L}_i\varphi_i(y_i) - \sum_{q=1}^{m} a_{qi}V_q(y_i) - f_i(y_i) \geq 0. \tag{4.2.7}$$

By the definition of V_i, we have

$$V_i(y_i) - g_i(y_i) \geq 0. \tag{4.2.8}$$

From (4.2.7) and (4.2.8), we see that V_i is a viscosity supersolution of the variational inequality (4.2.2).

(3) *The viscosity subsolution property.* Fix an $i \in \{1, 2, \cdots, m\}$. Suppose that $\varphi_i \in C^2(\mathbb{R})$ and $V_i - \varphi_i$ has a maximum at some point $\bar{y}_i \in \mathbb{R}$ such that $V_i(\bar{y}_i) = \varphi_i(\bar{y}_i)$. We will prove that V_i is a viscosity subsolution of the variational inequality (4.2.2) by contradiction.

Suppose that

$$rV_i(\bar{y}_i) - \mathcal{L}_i\varphi_i(\bar{y}_i) - \sum_{q=1}^{m} a_{qi}V_q(\bar{y}_i) - f_i(\bar{y}_i) > 0,$$

and

$$V_i(\bar{y}_i) - g_i(\bar{y}_i) > 0.$$

Hence for any positive number ε small enough and k large enough, thanks to the continuity of the functions $\mathcal{L}_i\varphi_i(\cdot)$, $f_i(\cdot)$ and $V_j(\cdot)$, where $j = 1, 2, \cdots, m$, there is a positive number ρ such that

$$r\varphi_i(y) - \mathcal{L}_i\varphi_i(y) - \sum_{q=1}^{m} a_{qi}\varphi_q^k(y) - f_i(y) > \varepsilon \text{ for } y \in (\bar{y}_i - \rho, \bar{y}_i + \rho),$$

and

$$\varphi_i(y) - g_i(y) > \varepsilon \text{ for } y \in (\bar{y}_i - \rho, \bar{y}_i + \rho).$$

Consequently, for $X(0) = e_i$, $Y(0) = \bar{y}_i$, defining $\delta := \inf\{t : t > 0, (X(t), Y(t)) \notin \{e_i\} \times (\bar{y}_i - \rho, \bar{y}_i + \rho)\}$, we have

$$r\varphi_i(Y(t)) - \mathcal{L}_i\varphi_i(Y(t)) - \sum_{q=1}^{m} a_{qi}\varphi_q^k(Y(t)) - f_i(Y(t)) > \varepsilon \text{ for } 0 \leq t \leq \delta, \tag{4.2.9}$$

and

(4.2.10)
$$\varphi_i(Y(t)) - g_i(Y(t)) > \varepsilon \text{ for } 0 \le t \le \delta.$$

.

For any stopping time $\tau \in \mathcal{T}$, by applying Itô's formula and noting (4.2.9) and (4.2.10), we obtain

(4.2.11)
$$\begin{aligned}
V_i(\bar{y}_i) &= \varphi_i(\bar{y}_i) \\
&= \mathbb{E}\Bigg[\int_0^{\delta\wedge\tau} \exp(-rt)\Big(r\varphi_i(Y(t)) - \mathcal{L}_i\varphi_i(Y(t)) - \sum_{q=1}^{m} a_{qi}\varphi_q^k(Y(t))\Big)\mathrm{d}t + \\
&\quad \sum_{j=1}^{m} \exp(-r(\delta\wedge\tau))\varphi_j^k(Y(\delta\wedge\tau))X_j(\delta\wedge\tau)\Bigg| X(0) = e_i, Y(0) = \bar{y}_i\Bigg] \\
&\ge \mathbb{E}\Bigg[\int_0^{\delta\wedge\tau} \exp(-rt)f(X(t),Y(t))\mathrm{d}t + \exp(-r\tau)g(X(\tau),Y(\tau))\mathbf{1}_{\{\delta>\tau\}} + \\
&\quad \exp(-r\delta)V(X(\delta),Y(\delta))\mathbf{1}_{\{\delta\le\tau\}}\Bigg| X(0) = e_i, Y(0) = \bar{y}_i\Bigg] + \\
&\quad \varepsilon\mathbb{E}\Bigg[\int_0^{\delta\wedge\tau} \exp(-rt)\mathrm{d}t + \exp(-r\tau)\mathbf{1}_{\{\delta>\tau\}}\Bigg| X(0) = e_i, Y(0) = \bar{y}_i\Bigg] - \frac{1}{k}.
\end{aligned}$$

We will show in Lemma 4.2.6 ahead that there is a positive constant C such that

$$\mathbb{E}\Bigg[\int_0^{\delta\wedge\tau} \exp(-rt)\mathrm{d}t + \exp(-r\tau)\mathbf{1}_{\{\delta>\tau\}}\Bigg| X(0) = e_i, Y(0) = \bar{y}_i\Bigg] \ge C.$$

Sending $k \to \infty$ and then taking supremum over $\tau \in \mathcal{T}$ in (4.2.11), we find

$$V_i(\bar{y}_i) \ge V_i(\bar{y}_i) + \varepsilon C,$$

which is a contradiction. Consequently, V_i is a viscosity subsolution of the variational inequality (4.2.2).

(4) *Uniqueness.* The proof of uniqueness is the same as that of [36, pp. 98–99, Uniqueness property]. Also refer to [16, pp. 31–32]. □

Lemma 4.2.6 *Using the notations introduced in the proof of Theorem 4.2.2, we have*

$$\mathbb{E}\left[\int_0^{\delta\wedge\tau} \exp(-rt)\mathrm{d}t + \exp(-r\tau)\mathbf{1}_{\{\delta>\tau\}}\middle| X(0)=e_i, Y(0)=\bar{y}_i\right] \geq C$$

for some positive constant C.

Proof. (1) Let Y_i be the solution of the equation

$$\mathrm{d}Y_i(t) = \alpha_i(Y_i(t))\mathrm{d}t + \beta_i(Y_i(t))\mathrm{d}B(t), \quad Y_i(0) = \bar{y}_i.$$

Define $T_{\bar{y}_i} := \inf\{t : t > 0, |Y_i(t) - \bar{y}_i| = \rho\}$. Since $\beta_i(\cdot) > 0$, we have, by [29, p. 152, Corollary 6.12.2],

$$\mathbb{P}(T_{\bar{y}_i} < +\infty | Y_i(0) = \bar{y}_i) > 0. \tag{4.2.12}$$

(2) Define $T := \inf\{t : t > 0, X(t) \neq e_i\}$. Thanks to the independence of X and B, it follows that

$$\begin{aligned}&\mathbb{P}(\exists t \in (0,T), \text{ s.t. } |Y(t) - \bar{y}_i| = \rho | X(0) = e_i, Y(0) = \bar{y}_i)\\ =& \int_0^{+\infty} \mathbb{P}(\exists s \in (0,t), \text{ s.t. } |Y_i(s) - \bar{y}_i| = \rho | Y(0) = \bar{y}_i)(-a_{ii}\exp(a_{ii}t))\mathrm{d}t,\end{aligned}$$

where we have used the fact that $\mathbb{P}(T > t | X(0) = e_i) = \exp(a_{ii}t)$.

The above equality and (4.2.12) yield

$$\mathbb{P}(\exists t \in (0,T), \text{ s.t. } |Y(t) - \bar{y}_i| = \rho | X(0) = e_i, Y(0) = \bar{y}_i) > 0.$$

Consequently, we obtain

$$\mathbb{E}\left[|Y(\delta) - \bar{y}_i|^2 \middle| X(0) = e_i, Y(0) = \bar{y}_i\right] > 0. \tag{4.2.13}$$

(3) Set $B_i := (\bar{y}_i - \rho, \bar{y}_i + \rho)$ and

$$C_1 := \min\left\{\left(r + \frac{2}{\rho}\sup_{y\in B_i}|\alpha(e_i,y)| + \frac{1}{\rho^2}\sup_{y\in B_i}\beta(e_i,y)^2\right)^{-1}, 1\right\}.$$

Define a function $G : B_i \to \mathbb{R}$ by

$$G(y) := C_1\left(1 - \frac{|y - \bar{y}_i|^2}{\rho^2}\right).$$

Then we have

$$\begin{aligned}
&\mathbb{E}\left[\int_0^{\delta\wedge\tau}\exp(-rt)\mathrm{d}t+\exp(-r\tau)\mathbf{1}_{\{\delta>\tau\}}\middle|X(0)=e_i,Y(0)=\bar{y}_i\right]\\
\geq\ &\mathbb{E}\left[\int_0^{\delta\wedge\tau}\exp(-rt)\Big(rG(Y(t))-\mathcal{L}_iG(Y(t))\Big)\mathrm{d}t+\right.\\
&\exp(-r\delta\wedge\tau)G(Y(\delta\wedge\tau))-\\
&\left.\exp(-r\delta)G(Y(\delta))\mathbf{1}_{\{\delta\leq\tau\}}\middle|X(0)=e_i,Y(0)=\bar{y}_i\right]\\
=\ &G(\bar{y}_i)-\mathbb{E}\left[\exp(-r\delta)G(Y(\delta))\mathbf{1}_{\{\delta\leq\tau\}}\middle|\,X(0)=e_i,Y(0)=\bar{y}_i\right]\\
\geq\ &C_1\rho^{-2}\mathbb{E}\left[|Y(\delta)-\bar{y}_i|^2\middle|\,X(0)=e_i,Y(0)=\bar{y}_i\right]=:C>0,
\end{aligned}$$

where we have used the facts $rG(y)-\mathcal{L}_iG(y)\leq 1$ and $G(y)\leq 1$ for the first inequality, Itô's formula for the first equality, and (4.2.13) for the last inequality. The proof is complete. □

We will prove that V is uniquely determined by the system (4.2.2). To do this, we introduce some notations.

Set $\mu_i:=\limsup\limits_{x\to\infty}\left|\frac{\alpha_i(x)}{x}\right|$ and $\sigma_i:=\limsup\limits_{x\to\infty}\left|\frac{\beta_i(x)}{x}\right|$, $i=1,2,\cdots,m$. Then we define the functions $w_i(\lambda):=r-a_{ii}-\mu_i\lambda-\frac{1}{2}\sigma_i^2\lambda(\lambda-1)$, $i=1,2,\cdots,m$, and a matrix $H(\lambda):=(h_{ij}(\lambda))_{m\times m}$, where $h_{ii}:=w_i$ and $h_{ij}:=-a_{ij}$ for $i\neq j$.

We make the following hypothesis.

(H1) There are positive numbers b_i such that $\sum\limits_{i=1}^{m}b_ih_{ij}(\overline{\lambda})\geq 0$ for some constant $\overline{\lambda}>1$, $j=1,2,\cdots,m$.

Theorem 4.2.7 *Assume that* (H1) *holds. Let* $\{U_i\}_{i=1}^m$ *be a family of functions defined on* $\mathbb{R}$ *with at most linear growth such that for each fixed* i*,* U_i *is a viscosity solution of*

$$\min\left\{rU_i-\mathcal{L}_iU_i-\sum_{q=1}^{m}a_{qi}U_q-f_i,U_i-g_i\right\}=0 \text{ on } \mathbb{R}.$$

Then $U_i=V_i$ *for* $i=1,2,\cdots,m$.

Proof. (1) Since U_i and V_i, $i=1,2,\cdots,m$, grow at most linearly, we have

$$\lim_{x\to\infty}(U_i(x)-V_i(x)-b_i|x|^{\overline{\lambda}})=-\infty,\ i=1,2,\cdots,m.$$

(2) Thanks to (H1), there is a positive constant K such that, for each $i = 1, 2, \cdots, m$,

$$\min\left\{ r\widetilde{\psi}_i - \mathcal{L}_i\widetilde{\psi}_i - \sum_{q=1}^{m} a_{qi}\widetilde{\psi}_q, \widetilde{\psi}_i - g_i \right\} \geq 0 \text{ on } \mathbb{R} \setminus [-K, K],$$

where $\widetilde{\psi}_i(x) := b_i|x|^{\overline{\lambda}}$.

Choose some functions $\overline{\psi}_i \in C^2(\mathbb{R})$ satisfying $\overline{\psi}_i|_{\mathbb{R}\setminus[-K,K]} = \widetilde{\psi}_i$, $i = 1, 2, \cdots, m$. Then it follows that

$$\min\left\{ r\psi_i - \mathcal{L}_i\psi_i - \sum_{q=1}^{m} a_{qi}\psi_q, \psi_i - g_i \right\} \geq 0 \text{ on } \mathbb{R},$$

where $\psi_i(x) := C + \overline{\psi}_i(x)$, $i = 1, 2, \cdots, m$, for some constant C large enough.

(3) Define $V_i^\varepsilon := V_i + \varepsilon\psi_i$ for $\varepsilon \in (0, 1)$ and $i = 1, 2, \cdots, m$. Then V_i^ε is a viscosity supersolution of

$$\min\left\{ rV_i^\varepsilon - \mathcal{L}_iV_i^\varepsilon - \sum_{q=1}^{m} a_{qi}V_q^\varepsilon - f_i, V_i^\varepsilon - g_i \right\} = 0 \text{ on } \mathbb{R}.$$

(4) We prove $U_i \leq V_i^\varepsilon$, $i = 1, 2, \cdots, m$, by contradiction. Otherwise, we have by Step 1

$$\begin{aligned} M :&= \max_{i\in\{1,\cdots,m\}} \sup_{x\in\mathbb{R}}\{U_i(x) - V_i^\varepsilon(x)\} \\ &= \max_{x\in\mathbb{R}}\{U_k(x) - V_k^\varepsilon(x)\} = U_k(\hat{x}) - V_k^\varepsilon(\hat{x}) > 0 \end{aligned} \tag{4.2.14}$$

for some $k \in \{1, 2, \cdots, m\}$ and $\hat{x} \in \mathbb{R}$.

For each positive integer $n \in \mathbb{N}$, we define a function $\varPhi_n$ by

$$\varPhi_n(x, y) := U_k(x) - V_k^\varepsilon(y) - \frac{n}{2}(x - y)^2.$$

In virtue of Step 1, we take $\mathcal{O} := (-R, R)$ with $U_k(x) - V_k^\varepsilon(x) < 0$ for all $|x| \geq R$. Then $\varPhi_n$ has a maximum point (x_n, y_n) on $\overline{\mathcal{O}}$. By the similar argument to the step 1 of the proof of [36, p. 77, Theorem 4.4.4], we have, up to a subsequence,

(4.2.15)

$$\lim_{n\to\infty} \varPhi_n(x_n, y_n) = M, \lim_{n\to\infty} n(x_n - y_n)^2 = 0 \text{ and } \lim_{n\to\infty} x_n = \lim_{n\to\infty} y_n = \hat{x}.$$

Therefore, for n large enough, (x_n, y_n) is a local maximum point of Φ_n relative to $\mathcal{O}$. Consequently, according to [16, p. 17, p. 19], there are two constants a and b with $a \le b$ such that

$$(n(x_n - y_n), a) \in \overline{J}_{\mathcal{O}}^{2,+} U_k(x_n), \ (n(x_n - y_n), b) \in \overline{J}_{\mathcal{O}}^{2,-} V_k(x_n),$$

and

$$a\beta_k(x_n)^2 - b\beta_k(y_n)^2 \le 3n(\beta_k(x_n) - \beta_k(y_n))^2. \tag{4.2.16}$$

Then, in light of the viscosity property of U_k and V_k^ε, it follows that

$$\min\Big\{rU_k(x_n) - \alpha_k(x_n)(n(x_n - y_n)) - \frac{a}{2}\beta_k(x_n)^2 - \sum_{q=1}^m a_{qk}U_q(x_n) - f_k(x_n), U_k(x_n) - g_k(x_n)\Big\} \le 0, \tag{4.2.17}$$

and

$$\min\Big\{rV_k^\varepsilon(y_n) - \alpha_k(y_n)(n(x_n - y_n)) - \frac{b}{2}\beta_k(y_n)^2 - \sum_{q=1}^m a_{qk}V_q^\varepsilon(y_n) - f_k(y_n), V_k^\varepsilon(y_n) - g_k(y_n)\Big\} \ge 0. \tag{4.2.18}$$

`Case 1` $U_k(x_n) - g_k(x_n) > 0$ for all n large enough.
Subtracting (4.2.18) from (4.2.17) yileds

$$r(U_k(x_n) - V_k^\varepsilon(y_n)) \le n(\alpha_k(x_n) - \alpha_k(y_n))(x_n - y_n) + \frac{a}{2}\beta_k(x_n)^2 - \frac{b}{2}\beta_k(y_n)^2 + \sum_{q=1}^m a_{qk}(U_q(x_n) - V_q^\varepsilon(y_n)) + f_k(x_n) - f_k(y_n)$$

for all n large enough.

Note (4.2.15), (4.2.16) and the Lipschitz continuity of the functions α_k, β_k and f_k. By taking limits in the above inequality as $n \to +\infty$, it follows that

$$r(U_k(\hat{x}) - V_k^\varepsilon(\hat{x})) \le \sum_{q=1}^m a_{qk}(U_q(\hat{x}) - V_q^\varepsilon(\hat{x})).$$

Therefore, in light of (4.2.14) and $\sum\limits_{q=1}^{m} a_{qk} = 0$, we have $rM \leq 0$, which is a contradiction.

`Case 2` $U_k(x_n) - g_k(x_n) \leq 0$ frequently.

In this case, the following inequality

$$U_k(x_n) - V_k^{\varepsilon}(y_n) \leq g_k(x_n) - g_k(y_n)$$

holds frequently.

Then, using the continuity of the function g_k, we get $M \leq 0$, which is a contradiction.

In conclusion, we have proved $U_i \leq V_i^{\varepsilon}$, $i = 1, 2, \cdots, m$.

(5) Taking limits in $U_i \leq V_i^{\varepsilon}$, $i = 1, 2, \cdots, m$, as $\varepsilon \to 0^+$, we have $U_i \leq V_i$, $i = 1, 2, \cdots, m$.

(6) Similarly, $U_i \geq V_i$, $i = 1, 2, \cdots, m$. This and Step 5 imply $U_i = V_i$, $i = 1, 2, \cdots, m$. □

Corollary 4.2.8 *Assume that*

$$r > \max\{\mu_1, \mu_2, \cdots, \mu_m\}. \tag{4.2.19}$$

Let $\{U_i\}_{i=1}^m$ be a family of functions defined on $\mathbb{R}$ with at most linear growth such that for each i, U_i is a viscosity solution of

$$\min\left\{rU_i - \mathcal{L}_i U_i - \sum_{q=1}^{m} a_{qi} U_q - f_i, U_i - g_i\right\} = 0 \text{ on } \mathbb{R}.$$

Then $U_i = V_i$ for $i = 1, 2, \cdots, m$.

Proof. Noting that $\sum\limits_{i=1}^{m} a_{ij} = 0$, $j = 1, 2, \cdots, m$, we have $\sum\limits_{i=1}^{m} h_{ij}(\lambda) = r - \mu_j\lambda - \sigma_j^2\lambda(\lambda - 1)$. This and (4.2.19) yield (H1). □

Let us introduce some notations as follows.

$$\mathcal{C}_i := \{y : V_i(y) > g_i(y)\},$$

$$\mathcal{S}_i := \{y : V_i(y) = g_i(y)\},$$

$$\mathcal{D}_i := \left\{ y : rg_i(y) - \mathcal{L}_i g_i(y) - \sum_{q=1}^{m} a_{qi} g_q(y) - f_i(y) \geq 0 \right\},$$

and

$$\widehat{V}_i(y) := \mathbb{E}\left[\int_0^{\infty} \exp(-rt) f(X(t), Y(t)) \mathrm{d}t \,\middle|\, X(0) = e_i, Y(0) = y \right],$$

for each $i = 1, 2, \cdots, m$.

We consider the regularity of V in the following theorem.

Theorem 4.2.9 *The function V_i is C^2 continuous on $\mathcal{C}_i$ and C^1 continuous on $\partial\mathcal{C}_i$, $i = 1, 2, \cdots, m$.*

Proof. It follows from $\beta(\cdot, \cdot) > 0$ that $\mathcal{L}_i$ is locally elliptic. Then, thanks to Theorem 4.2.2, the proof is completed in the same way as that of [36, p. 100, Lemma 5.2.2, Proposition 5.2.1]. □

Theorem 4.2.10 *The stopping time $\tau^* := \inf \left\{ t > 0 : (X(t), Y(t)) \in \bigcup_{i=1}^{m} \{e_i\} \times \mathcal{S}_i \right\}$ is an optimal stopping time of the problem* (4.2.1).

Proof. We refer to [36, pp. 101–102] for the proof. □

Theorem 4.2.11 states some properties about $\mathcal{S}_i$.

Theorem 4.2.11 *Assume that* (H1) *holds. Then the following conclusions are true.*

① *If $\bigcup_{i=1}^{m} \mathcal{S}_i = \emptyset$, then $\widehat{V}_i \geq g_i$ for each $i = 1, 2, \cdots, m$.*

② *If $\widehat{V}_i \geq g_i$ for each $i = 1, 2, \cdots, m$, then $V_i = \widehat{V}_i$.*

③ *If g_i is C^2 continuous for some $i \in \{1, 2, \cdots, m\}$, then $\mathcal{S}_i$ is included in $\mathcal{D}_i$.*

Proof. By virtue of Theorem 4.2.7, ① and ② are proved in a similar way to that of [36, p. 102, Lemma 5.2.3]; for the proof of ③, we apply Theorem 4.2.7 and refer to [36, p. 102, Lemma 5.2.4]. □

Now we study the form of $\mathcal{S}_i$. To do this, we make the following assumption.

(H2) The process Y takes values in $(0,+\infty)$ and $|\alpha_i(y)|+|\beta_i(y)|\le C|y|$ for some constant C, $i=1,2,\cdots,m$.

We will use the fact that the matrix $rI_{m\times m}-(a_{ij})_{m\times m}$ is invertible. This follows from that $rI_{m\times m}-(a_{ij})_{m\times m}$ is a strictly diagonally dominant matrix, since $r>0$ and $\sum\limits_{i=1}^{m}a_{ij}=0$ for all $j=1,2,\cdots,m$. Let $(b_{ij})_{m\times m}$ denote the inverse of $rI_{m\times m}-(a_{ij})_{m\times m}$.

Since V_i is Lipschitz continuous, it is reasonable to set $V_i(0):=V_i(0^+)$.

Lemma 4.2.12 *Assume that* (H2) *holds. Then*

$$V_i(0)=\max\left\{\sum_{q=1}^{m}b_{qi}f_q(0),g_i(0)\right\},\quad i=1,2,\cdots,m.$$

Proof. By taking limits as $y\to 0^+$, Theorem 4.2.2 implies that $V_i(0)$ is a solution of

$$\min\left\{rV_i(0)-\sum_{q=1}^{m}a_{qi}V_q(0)-f_i(0),V_i(0)-g_i(0)\right\}=0.$$

Consequently, $V_i(0)=\max\left\{\sum\limits_{q=1}^{m}b_{qi}f_q(0),g_i(0)\right\}$. This completes the proof. □

Theorem 4.2.13 *Assume that* (H1) *and* (H2) *hold, all $\mathcal{S}_i$ are nonempty connected sets, and all g_i are C^2 continuous. Then the following are true.*

① *If $\mathcal{D}_i=[a_i,+\infty)$ for some positive constant a_i, $i=1,2,\cdots,m$, then $\mathcal{S}_i=[\inf\mathcal{S}_i,+\infty)$.*

② *If $g_i(0)>\sum\limits_{i=1}^{m}b_{qi}f_q(0)$ and $\mathcal{D}_i=(0,b_i]$ for some positive constant b_i, $i=1,2,\cdots,m$, then $\mathcal{S}_i=(0,\sup\mathcal{S}_i]$.*

Proof. Set $a_i^*:=\inf\mathcal{S}_i$ in Case ① and $b_i^*:=\sup\mathcal{S}_i$ in Case ②. Then we define $A_i:=[a_i^*,+\infty)$ in Case ① and $A_i:=(0,b_i^*]$ in Case ②. We will prove $\mathcal{S}_i=A_i$.

Note the following facts:

- g_i grows at most linearly;
- $g_i(a_i^*)=V_i(a_i^*)$ or $g_i(b_i^*)=V_i(b_i^*)$ by the continuity of g_i and V_i;
- in light of Lemma 4.2.12, $g_i(0)=V_i(0)$ if $g_i(0)>\sum\limits_{i=1}^{m}b_{qi}f_q(0)$.

Moreover, thanks to $A_i \subset \mathcal{D}_i$ by Theorem 4.2.11, g_i solves the inequality

$$rg_i - \mathcal{L}_i g_i - \sum_{q=1}^{m} a_{qi} g_q - f_i \geq 0 \text{ on } A_i.$$

Thus, by Theorem 4.2.7, it follows that $g_i = V_i$ on A_i. The proof is complete. □

4.3 An application

A firm is extracting a kind of natural resource (oil, gas, etc.). We will determine what time is optimal to stop the extraction.

Let $(\Omega, \mathscr{F}, \{\mathscr{F}_t\}_{t\geq 0}, \mathbb{P})$ be a filtered probability space. We assume that $\{\mathscr{F}_t\}_{t\geq 0}$ satisfies the usual conditions and $\mathscr{F}_0$ is the completion of $\{\emptyset, \Omega\}$.

Let $X := (X(t), t \geq 0)$ be a time homogeneous Markov chain defined on $(\Omega, \mathscr{F}, \{\mathscr{F}_t\}_{t\geq 0}, \mathbb{P})$ taking values in the standard orthogonal basis of $\mathbb{R}^2$, $I := \{e_1, e_2\}$, with a rate matrix $A := \begin{bmatrix} -\lambda_1 & \lambda_2 \\ \lambda_1 & -\lambda_2 \end{bmatrix}$ for some positive constants λ_1 and λ_2.

Let $B(t)$ be a one dimensional standard Brownian motion, which is independent of X, defined on $(\Omega, \mathscr{F}, \{\mathscr{F}_t\}_{t\geq 0}, \mathbb{P})$.

We assume that the price process P of the resource satisfies

$$\text{(4.3.1)} \qquad \mathrm{d}P(t) = \mu(X(t))P(t)\mathrm{d}t + \sigma(X(t))P(t)\mathrm{d}B(t), \text{ and } P(0) > 0,$$

and set $\mu_i := \mu(e_i)$ and $\sigma_i := \sigma(e_i)$, $i = 1, 2$. We will assume that $\mu_1 \leq \mu_2$ and $\sigma_i > 0$, $i = 1, 2$.

Applying Itô's formula, we deduce that the solution of the equation (4.3.1) is

(4.3.2)

$$P(t) = P(0) \exp\left[\int_0^t \left(\mu(X(s)) - \frac{1}{2}\sigma(X(s))^2\right) \mathrm{d}s + \int_0^t \sigma(X(s))\mathrm{d}B(s)\right].$$

To answer what time is optimal to stop the extraction, we will solve the optimal problem

$$
\begin{aligned}
J_i(p) := \sup_{\tau\in\mathcal{T}} \mathbb{E}\bigg[\int_0^\tau & \exp(-rt)(P(t)-C)\mathrm{d}t - \\
& \exp(-r\tau)K\bigg|X(0)=e_i, P(0)=p\bigg],
\end{aligned} \tag{4.3.3}
$$

where $\mathcal{T}$ is the collection of all stopping times, r is the discount rate such that $r>0$, C is the running cost with $C>0$, and K is the cost at which the firm stops the extraction.

Lemma 4.3.1 (cf. [24, Lemma 1]) *We have*

$$
\mathbb{E}\left[\exp\left(\int_0^t \mu(X(s))\mathrm{d}s\right)\bigg| X(0)=e_i\right] = \frac{x_2-\mu_i}{x_2-x_1}\exp(x_1 t) + \frac{\mu_i - x_1}{x_2-x_1}\exp(x_2 t),
$$

where x_1 and x_2 are the solutions of

$$
x^2 + (\lambda_1-\mu_1+\lambda_2-\mu_2)x + (\lambda_1-\mu_1)(\lambda_2-\mu_2) - \lambda_1\lambda_2 = 0
$$

with $x_1 < x_2$.

Remark 4.3.2 If $\mu_1<\mu_2$, then $x_1<\mu_1<x_2<\mu_2$; if $\mu_1=\mu_2$, then $x_1 = \mu_1-\lambda_1-\lambda_2$ and $x_2=\mu_1$.

Theorem 4.3.3 *Assume $r\le x_2$. Then the optimal stopping time τ^* is given by $\tau^*=+\infty$ a.s., and the function J_i in (4.3.3) is given by $J_i(p)=+\infty$, $i=1,2$.*

Proof. By (4.3.2) and (4.3.3), we have, for fixed $T>0$,

$$
\begin{aligned}
J_i(p) \ge p\int_0^T \mathbb{E}\bigg[\exp(-rt)\exp\bigg(&\int_0^t \mu(X(s)) - \frac{1}{2}\sigma(X(s))^2\mathrm{d}s + \\
&\int_0^t \sigma(X(s))\mathrm{d}B(s)\bigg)\bigg| X(0)=e_i\bigg]\,\mathrm{d}t - \\
&r^{-1}[1-\exp(-rT)]C - \exp(-rT)K.
\end{aligned}
$$

Note that

$$
\left(\exp\left(\int_0^t \sigma(X(s))\mathrm{d}B(s) - \frac{1}{2}\int_0^t \sigma(X(s))^2\mathrm{d}s\right), t\ge 0\right)
$$

is a martingale. Then in light of the independence of X and B, we get

$$\begin{aligned}J_i(p) \geq p\int_0^T \exp(-rt)\mathbb{E}\left[\exp\left(\left(\int_0^t \mu(X(s))\right)\mathrm{d}s\middle| X(0)=e_i\right]\mathrm{d}t - \\ r^{-1}[1-\exp(-rT)]C - \exp(-rT)K \\ = p\left\{\frac{x_2-\mu_i}{x_2-x_1}\int_0^T \exp[(x_1-r)t]\mathrm{d}t + \frac{\mu_i - x_1}{x_2-x_1}\int_0^T \exp[(x_2-r)t]\mathrm{d}t\right\} - \\ r^{-1}[1-\exp(-rT)]C - \exp(-rT)K,\end{aligned}$$

where we have used Lemma 4.3.1.

Sending $T \to +\infty$ in the above inequality, we obtain $J_i(p) = +\infty$ since $r \leq x_2$. □

Corollary 4.3.4 *If $r \leq \mu_1$, then the conclusions in Theorem 4.3.3 hold.*

Proof. The proof can be completed by the fact that $r \leq \mu_1$ implies $r \leq x_2$. □

In the following discussion, we consider the case $r > x_2$.

Lemma 4.3.5 ① (cf. [25, Remark 2.1]) *The equation*

$$w_1(z)w_2(z) - \lambda_1\lambda_2 = 0,$$

where $w_i(z) := r+\lambda_i - \mu_i z - \frac{\sigma_i^2}{2}z(z-1)$, has four distinct solutions z_i satisfying $z_1 < z_2 < 0 < z_3 < z_4$ with $w_1(z_3) > 0$.

② *Assume that $r > x_2$. Then $z_3 > 1$ and there are positive constants b_i fulfilling $b_1 w_1(z_3) - \lambda_1 b_2 = 0$ and $b_2 w_2(z_3) - \lambda_2 b_1 = 0$. See Figure 4.1.*

Proof. (1) Set $Q(z) := w_1(z)w_2(z) - \lambda_1\lambda_2$. Note that the equation $w_1(z) = 0$ has two solutions, say, z^1 and z^2 with $z^1 < z^2$. Then $Q(z^i) < 0$, where $i = 1, 2$. In addition, we have $Q(0) > 0$ and $\lim\limits_{z\to\infty} Q(z) = +\infty$. Therefore, by the intermediate value theorem, it follows that the equation $w_1(z)w_2(z) - \lambda_1\lambda_2 = 0$ has four distinct solutions z_i satisfying $z_1 < z_2 < 0 < z_3 < z_4$. Furthermore, $w_1(z_3) > 0$, since $z^1 < z_3 < z^2$.

(2) Since $r > x_2$, we have

$$r^2 + (\lambda_1 - \mu_1 + \lambda_2 - \mu_2)r + (\lambda_1 - \mu_1)(\lambda_2 - \mu_2) - \lambda_1\lambda_2 > 0 \tag{4.3.4}$$

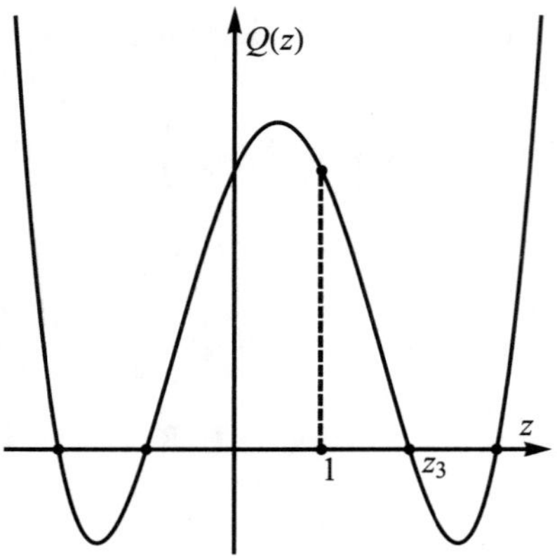

Figure 4.1 Solutions of $w_1(z)w_2(z) - \lambda_1\lambda_2 = 0$

and

$$2r + \lambda_1 - \mu_1 + \lambda_2 - \mu_2 > 0. \tag{4.3.5}$$

Then it follows from (4.3.4) that $Q(1) > 0$ and $(r+\lambda_1-\mu_1)(r+\lambda_2-\mu_2) > 0$. Combining (4.3.5) and $(r+\lambda_1-\mu_1)(r+\lambda_2-\mu_2) > 0$, we have $r+\lambda_1-\mu_1 > 0$ and $r+\lambda_2-\mu_2 > 0$.

(3) In this step, we prove $z_3 > 1$.

`Case 1` $\mu_i + \sigma_i^2/2 > 0$, where $i = 1, 2$.

In this case, we have

$$Q'(1) = -(r+\lambda_1-\mu_1)\left(\mu_2 + \frac{\sigma_2^2}{2}\right) - (r+\lambda_2-\mu_2)\left(\mu_1 + \frac{\sigma_1^2}{2}\right) < 0.$$

This and $Q(1) > 0$ imply $z_3 > 1$.

`Case 2` $\mu_i + \sigma_i^2/2 < 0$, where $i = 1, 2$.

In this case, we have

$$Q'''(1) = 3\sigma_1^2\sigma_2^2 + 3(\sigma_1^2\mu_2 + \sigma_2^2\mu_1) < 0.$$

This and $Q(1) > 0$ imply $z_3 > 1$.

`Case 3` $(\mu_1 + \sigma_1^2/2)(\mu_2 + \sigma_2^2/2) \le 0$.

In this case, we have

$$Q''(1) = -\sigma_1^2(r+\lambda_2-\mu_2) + 2\left(\mu_1 + \frac{\sigma_1^2}{2}\right)\left(\mu_2 + \frac{\sigma_2^2}{2}\right) - \sigma_1^2(r+\lambda_2-\mu_2) < 0.$$

This and $Q(1) > 0$ imply $z_3 > 1$.

(4) Take $b_1 = 1$ and $b_2 = w_1(z_3)/\lambda_1$. Then we have $b_1 w_1(z_3) - \lambda_1 b_2 = 0$ and $b_2 w_2(z_3) - \lambda_2 b_1 = 0$. □

Lemma 4.3.6 *Assume that $r > x_2$. Then J_i is a Lipschitz continuous function, $i = 1, 2$. In addition, $\mathcal{S}_i := \{p : p \in (0, +\infty)$ and $J_i(p) = -K\}$ is connected, $i = 1, 2$.*

Proof. (1) By (4.3.2) and (4.3.3), we have

$$\begin{aligned}&|J_i(p_1) - J_i(p_2)|\\ \le\ & |p_1 - p_2| \int_0^{+\infty} \mathbb{E}\left[\exp(-rt)\exp\left(\int_0^t \mu(X(s)) - \frac{1}{2}\sigma(X(s))^2 \mathrm{d}s + \right.\right.\\ & \left.\left.\left.\int_0^t \sigma(X(s))\mathrm{d}B(s)\right)\right| X(0) = e_i\right] \mathrm{d}t.\end{aligned}$$

Note that

$$\left(\exp\left(\int_0^t \sigma(X(s))\mathrm{d}B(s) - \frac{1}{2}\int_0^t \sigma(X(s))^2 \mathrm{d}s\right), t \ge 0\right)$$

is a martingale. Then in light of the independence of X and B, we get

$$\begin{aligned}&|J_i(p_1) - J_i(p_2)|\\ \le\ & |p_1 - p_2| \int_0^{+\infty} \exp(-rt)\mathbb{E}\left[\exp\left(\int_0^t \mu(X(s))\right) \mathrm{d}s \,\middle|\, X(0) = e_i\right] \mathrm{d}t\\ =\ & \frac{1}{x_2 - x_1}\left(\frac{x_2 - \mu_i}{r - x_1} + \frac{\mu_i - x_1}{r - x_2}\right)|p_1 - p_2|,\end{aligned}$$

where we have used Lemma 4.3.1 and $r > x_2$ for the equality.

(2) We prove that $\mathcal{S}_i := \{p : p \in (0, +\infty)$ and $J_i(p) = -K\}$ is connected by contradiction. Suppose that $a, b \in \mathcal{S}_i$ but there is a point $c \in (a, b)$ with $c \notin \mathcal{S}_i$ (i.e., $J_i(c) > -K$).

Noting that J_i is convex, we have

$$J_i(c) \le \frac{b - c}{b - a} J_i(a) + \frac{c - a}{b - a} J_i(b) = -K,$$

which contradicts $J_i(c) > -K$. □

Theorem 4.3.7 *Assume $r > x_2$. Then $\{J_1, J_2\}$ is the unique solution with at most linear growth of the variational inequalities*

$$\begin{cases} \min\Big\{(r+\lambda_1)J_1(p) - \mu_1 p J_1'(p) - \\ \quad \frac{1}{2}\sigma_1^2 p^2 J_1''(p) - \lambda_1 J_2(p) - p + C, J_1(p) + K\Big\} = 0 \\ \min\Big\{(r+\lambda_2)J_2(p) - \mu_2 p J_2'(p) - \\ \quad \frac{1}{2}\sigma_2^2 p^2 J_2''(p) - \lambda_2 J_1(p) - p + C, J_2(p) + K\Big\} = 0 \end{cases}$$

with boundary condition $J_i(0) = -\min\{C/r, K\}$, $i = 1, 2$, on $(0, +\infty)$ in viscosity sense .

Proof. It follows from Lemma 4.2.12 that $J_i(0) = -\min\{C/r, K\}$, $i = 1, 2$. Then, by Lemma 4.3.5 and Lemma 4.3.6, the result is a straight corollary of Theorem 4.2.7. □

Remark 4.3.8 The boundary condition $J_i(0) = -\min\{C/r, K\}$, $i = 1, 2$, can also be obtained by (4.3.2) and (4.3.3). In fact,

$$\begin{aligned} J_i(0) &= \sup_{\tau\in\mathcal{T}} \mathbb{E}\left[\int_0^\tau \exp(-rt)(-C)\mathrm{d}t - \exp(-r\tau)K\right] \\ &= -\frac{C}{r} + \sup_{\tau\in\mathcal{T}} \mathbb{E}\left[\exp(-r\tau)\left(\frac{C}{r} - K\right)\right] \\ &= -\min\left\{\frac{C}{r}, K\right\}. \end{aligned}$$

Theorem 4.3.9 *Assume that $r > x_2$ and $C \le rK$. Then the optimal stopping time τ^* is given by $\tau^* = +\infty$ a.s.; furthermore, the functions J_i are given by*

$$J_1(p) = k_2 p - r^{-1}C, \ J_2(p) = k_1 p - r^{-1}C,$$

where

$$k_i = \frac{r+\lambda_1+\lambda_2-\mu_i}{(r+\lambda_1-\mu_1)(r+\lambda_2-\mu_2)-\lambda_1\lambda_2}, \ i = 1, 2.$$

Proof. Note that, for $i = 1, 2$,

$$\mathcal{S}_i \subset \{p : 0 < p \le C - rK\}$$

by Theorem 4.2.11. Thus we have $\mathcal{S}_i = \emptyset$.

Therefore, it follows from Theorem 4.3.7 that

$$J_1(p) = \frac{(r+\lambda_1+\lambda_2-\mu_2)p}{(r+\lambda_1-\mu_1)(r+\lambda_2-\mu_2)-\lambda_1\lambda_2} - \frac{C}{r}$$

and

$$J_2(p) = \frac{(r+\lambda_1+\lambda_2-\mu_1)p}{(r+\lambda_1-\mu_1)(r+\lambda_2-\mu_2)-\lambda_1\lambda_2} - \frac{C}{r}.$$

The proof is complete. □

Corollary 4.3.10 *If $r > \mu_2$ and $C \le rK$, then the conclusions in Theorem 4.3.9 hold.*

Proof. The proof can be completed by the fact that $r > \mu_2$ implies $r > x_2$. □

Recall that z_1 and z_2 are the solutions of $w_1(z)w_2(z) - \lambda_1\lambda_2 = 0$ with $z_1 < z_2 < 0$ (see Lemma 4.3.5).

Theorem 4.3.11 *Assume that $r > x_2$ and $C > rK$. Then one and only one of the following holds.*

① *The equation*

$$\begin{bmatrix} {p_1}^{-y_1} & 0 \\ 0 & {p_1}^{-y_2} \end{bmatrix}\begin{bmatrix} a_{11}p_1 + b_{11} \\ a_{21}p_1 + b_{21} \end{bmatrix} = \begin{bmatrix} {p_2}^{-y_1} & 0 \\ 0 & {p_2}^{-y_2} \end{bmatrix}\begin{bmatrix} a_{12}p_2 + b_{12} \\ a_{22}p_2 + b_{22} \end{bmatrix}$$

has a solution $\{p_1^*, p_2^*\}$ with $p_1^* < p_2^*$, where y_1 and y_2 are the two solutions of the quadratic equation

$$r + \lambda_1 - \mu_1 y - \frac{1}{2}\sigma_1^2 y(y-1) = 0$$

with $y_1 < y_2$,

$$\begin{bmatrix} a_{11} \\ a_{21} \end{bmatrix} = \begin{bmatrix} 1 & 1 \\ y_1 & y_2 \end{bmatrix}^{-1}\begin{bmatrix} \dfrac{-1}{r+\lambda_1-\mu_1} \\ \dfrac{-1}{r+\lambda_1-\mu_1} \end{bmatrix}, \quad \begin{bmatrix} b_{11} \\ b_{12} \end{bmatrix} = \begin{bmatrix} 1 & 1 \\ y_1 & y_2 \end{bmatrix}^{-1}\begin{bmatrix} \dfrac{C-rK}{r+\lambda_1} \\ 0 \end{bmatrix},$$

$$\begin{bmatrix} a_{12} \\ a_{22} \end{bmatrix} = \begin{bmatrix} 1 & 1 \\ y_1 & y_2 \end{bmatrix}^{-1} \left(\begin{bmatrix} k_2 - \dfrac{1}{r+\lambda_1-\mu_1} \\ k_2 - \dfrac{1}{r+\lambda_1-\mu_1} \end{bmatrix} - \lambda_1 \begin{bmatrix} 1 & 1 \\ z_1 & z_2 \end{bmatrix} \begin{bmatrix} w_1(z_1) & w_1(z_2) \\ w_1(z_1)z_1 & w_1(z_2)z_2 \end{bmatrix}^{-1} \begin{bmatrix} k_1 \\ k_1 \end{bmatrix} \right),$$

and

$$\begin{bmatrix} b_{12} \\ b_{22} \end{bmatrix} = \begin{bmatrix} 1 & 1 \\ y_1 & y_2 \end{bmatrix}^{-1} \left(\begin{bmatrix} \dfrac{\lambda_1 K + C}{r+\lambda_1} - \dfrac{C}{r} \\ 0 \end{bmatrix} + \lambda_1 \begin{bmatrix} 1 & 1 \\ z_1 & z_2 \end{bmatrix} \begin{bmatrix} w_1(z_1) & w_1(z_2) \\ w_1(z_1)z_1 & w_1(z_2)z_2 \end{bmatrix}^{-1} \begin{bmatrix} \dfrac{C-rK}{r} \\ 0 \end{bmatrix} \right).$$

In addition, the optimal stopping time τ^* is given by

$$\tau^* = \inf\{t : t > 0, (X(t), P(t)) \in \{e_1\} \times (0, p_1^*] \cup \{e_2\} \times (0, p_2^*]\},$$

and the functions J_i are given by

$$J_1(p) = \begin{cases} -K & \text{on } (0, p_1^*], \\ \dfrac{p}{r+\lambda_1-\mu_1} - \dfrac{\lambda_1 K + C}{r+\lambda_1} + A_1 p^{y_1} + A_2 p^{y_2} & \text{on } (p_1^*, p_2^*], \\ k_2 p - r^{-1}C + B_1 p^{z_1} + B_2 p^{z_2} & \text{on } (p_2^*, +\infty), \end{cases}$$

and

$$J_2(p) = \begin{cases} -K & \text{on } (0, p_2^*], \\ k_1 p - r^{-1}C + \lambda_1^{-1} w_1(z_1) B_1 p^{z_1} + \lambda_1^{-1} w_1(z_2) B_2 p^{z_2} & \text{on } (p_2^*, +\infty), \end{cases}$$

respectively. Here,

$$\begin{bmatrix} A_1 \\ A_2 \end{bmatrix} = \begin{bmatrix} p_1^{*-y_1} & 0 \\ 0 & p_1^{*-y_2} \end{bmatrix} \begin{bmatrix} a_{11}p_1^* + b_{11} \\ a_{21}p_1^* + b_{21} \end{bmatrix},$$

$$\begin{bmatrix} B_1 \\ B_2 \end{bmatrix} = \lambda_1 \begin{bmatrix} p_2^{*-z_1} & 0 \\ 0 & p_2^{*-z_2} \end{bmatrix} \begin{bmatrix} w_1(z_1) & w_1(z_2) \\ w_1(z_1)z_1 & w_1(z_2)z_2 \end{bmatrix}^{-1} \begin{bmatrix} -k_1 p_2^* + \dfrac{C-rK}{r} \\ -k_1 p_2^* \end{bmatrix}.$$

② *The equation*

$$\begin{bmatrix} p_2^{-\overline{y}_1} & 0 \\ 0 & p_2^{-\overline{y}_2} \end{bmatrix} \begin{bmatrix} \overline{a}_{11}p_2 + \overline{b}_{11} \\ \overline{a}_{21}p_2 + \overline{b}_{21} \end{bmatrix} = \begin{bmatrix} p_1^{-\overline{y}_1} & 0 \\ 0 & p_1^{-\overline{y}_2} \end{bmatrix} \begin{bmatrix} \overline{a}_{12}p_1 + \overline{b}_{12} \\ \overline{a}_{22}p_1 + \overline{b}_{22} \end{bmatrix}$$

has a solution $\{\overline{p}_1^*, \overline{p}_2^*\}$ *with* $\overline{p}_1^* > \overline{p}_2^*$, *where* $\overline{y}_1$ *and* $\overline{y}_2$ *are the two solutions of the quadratic equation*

$$r + \lambda_2 - \mu_2 y - \frac{1}{2}\sigma_2^2 y(y-1) = 0$$

with $\overline{y}_1 < \overline{y}_2$,

$$\begin{bmatrix} \overline{a}_{11} \\ \overline{a}_{21} \end{bmatrix} = \begin{bmatrix} 1 & 1 \\ \overline{y}_1 & \overline{y}_2 \end{bmatrix}^{-1} \begin{bmatrix} \dfrac{-1}{r+\lambda_2-\mu_2} \\ \dfrac{-1}{r+\lambda_2-\mu_2} \end{bmatrix}, \quad \begin{bmatrix} \overline{b}_{11} \\ \overline{b}_{12} \end{bmatrix} = \begin{bmatrix} 1 & 1 \\ \overline{y}_1 & \overline{y}_2 \end{bmatrix}^{-1} \begin{bmatrix} \dfrac{C-rK}{r+\lambda_2} \\ 0 \end{bmatrix},$$

$$\begin{bmatrix} \overline{a}_{12} \\ \overline{a}_{22} \end{bmatrix} = \begin{bmatrix} 1 & 1 \\ \overline{y}_1 & \overline{y}_2 \end{bmatrix}^{-1} \left(\begin{bmatrix} k_1 - \dfrac{1}{r+\lambda_2-\mu_2} \\ k_1 - \dfrac{1}{r+\lambda_2-\mu_2} \end{bmatrix} - \lambda_2 \begin{bmatrix} 1 & 1 \\ z_1 & z_2 \end{bmatrix} \begin{bmatrix} w_2(z_1) & w_2(z_2) \\ w_2(z_1)z_1 & w_2(z_2)z_2 \end{bmatrix}^{-1} \begin{bmatrix} k_2 \\ k_2 \end{bmatrix} \right),$$

and

$$\begin{bmatrix} \overline{b}_{12} \\ \overline{b}_{22} \end{bmatrix} = \begin{bmatrix} 1 & 1 \\ \overline{y}_1 & \overline{y}_2 \end{bmatrix}^{-1} \left(\begin{bmatrix} \dfrac{\lambda_2 K + C}{r+\lambda_2} - \dfrac{C}{r} \\ 0 \end{bmatrix} + \lambda_2 \begin{bmatrix} 1 & 1 \\ z_1 & z_2 \end{bmatrix} \begin{bmatrix} w_2(z_1) & w_2(z_2) \\ w_2(z_1)z_1 & w_2(z_2)z_2 \end{bmatrix}^{-1} \begin{bmatrix} \dfrac{C-rK}{r} \\ 0 \end{bmatrix} \right).$$

In addition, the optimal stopping time τ^* *is given by*

$$\tau^* = \inf\{t : t > 0, (X(t), P(t)) \in \{e_1\} \times (0, \overline{p}_1^*] \cup \{e_2\} \times (0, \overline{p}_2^*]\},$$

and the functions J_i *are given by*

$$J_1(p) = \begin{cases} -K & \text{on } (0, \overline{p}_1^*], \\ k_2 p - r^{-1}C + \lambda_2^{-1} w_2(z_1)\overline{B}_1 p^{z_1} + \lambda_2^{-1} w_2(z_2)\overline{B}_2 p^{z_2} & \text{on } (\overline{p}_1^*, +\infty), \end{cases}$$

and

$$J_2(p) = \begin{cases} -K & \text{on } (0, \overline{p}_2^*], \\ \dfrac{p}{r+\lambda_2-\mu_2} - \dfrac{\lambda_2 K + C}{r+\lambda_2} + \overline{A}_1 p^{\overline{y}_1} + \overline{A}_2 p^{\overline{y}_2} & \text{on } (\overline{p}_2^*, \overline{p}_1^*], \\ k_1 p - r^{-1}C + \overline{B}_1 p^{z_1} + \overline{B}_2 p^{z_2} & \text{on } (\overline{p}_1^*, +\infty), \end{cases}$$

respectively. Here,

$$\begin{bmatrix} \overline{A}_1 \\ \overline{A}_2 \end{bmatrix} = \begin{bmatrix} \overline{p}_2^{*-y_1} & 0 \\ 0 & \overline{p}_2^{*-y_2} \end{bmatrix} \begin{bmatrix} \overline{a}_{11}\overline{p}_1^* + \overline{b}_{11} \\ \overline{a}_{21}\overline{p}_1^* + \overline{b}_{21} \end{bmatrix},$$

$$\begin{bmatrix} \overline{B}_1 \\ \overline{B}_2 \end{bmatrix} = \lambda_2 \begin{bmatrix} \overline{p}_1^{*-z_1} & 0 \\ 0 & \overline{p}_1^{*-z_2} \end{bmatrix} \begin{bmatrix} w_2(z_1) & w_2(z_2) \\ w_2(z_1)z_1 & w_2(z_2)z_2 \end{bmatrix}^{-1} \begin{bmatrix} -k_2\overline{p}_1^* + \dfrac{C-rK}{r} \\ -k_2\overline{p}_1^* \end{bmatrix}.$$

③ *The equation*

$$\begin{bmatrix} \widetilde{a}_{11}p + \widetilde{b}_{11} \\ \widetilde{a}_{21}p + \widetilde{b}_{21} \end{bmatrix} = \begin{bmatrix} \widetilde{a}_{12}p + \widetilde{b}_{12} \\ \widetilde{a}_{22}p + \widetilde{b}_{22} \end{bmatrix}$$

has a positive solution p^*, where

$$\begin{bmatrix} \widetilde{a}_{11} \\ \widetilde{a}_{12} \end{bmatrix} = \begin{bmatrix} 1 & 1 \\ z_1 & z_2 \end{bmatrix}^{-1} \begin{bmatrix} -k_2 \\ -k_2 \end{bmatrix}, \quad \begin{bmatrix} \widetilde{b}_{11} \\ \widetilde{b}_{12} \end{bmatrix} = \begin{bmatrix} 1 & 1 \\ z_1 & z_2 \end{bmatrix}^{-1} \begin{bmatrix} \dfrac{C-rK}{r} \\ 0 \end{bmatrix},$$

$$\begin{bmatrix} \widetilde{a}_{12} \\ \widetilde{a}_{22} \end{bmatrix} = \lambda_1 \begin{bmatrix} w_1(z_1) & w_1(z_2) \\ w_1(z_1)z_1 & w_1(z_2)z_2 \end{bmatrix}^{-1} \begin{bmatrix} -k_1 \\ -k_1 \end{bmatrix},$$

and

$$\begin{bmatrix} \widetilde{b}_{12} \\ \widetilde{b}_{22} \end{bmatrix} = \lambda_1 \begin{bmatrix} w_1(z_1) & w_1(z_2) \\ w_1(z_1)z_1 & w_1(z_2)z_2 \end{bmatrix}^{-1} \begin{bmatrix} \dfrac{C-rK}{r} \\ 0 \end{bmatrix}.$$

In addition, the optimal stopping time τ^* is given by

$$\tau^* = \inf\{t : t > 0, P(t) \in (0, p^*]\},$$

and the functions J_i are given by

$$J_1(p) = \begin{cases} -K & \text{on } (0, p^*], \\ k_2 p - r^{-1}C + \widetilde{B}_1 p^{z_1} + \widetilde{B}_2 p^{z_2} & \text{on } (p^*, +\infty), \end{cases}$$

and

$$J_2(p) = \begin{cases} -K & \text{on } (0, p^*], \\ k_1 p - r^{-1}C + \lambda_1^{-1} w_1(z_1)\widetilde{B}_1 p^{z_1} + \lambda_1^{-1} w_1(z_2)\widetilde{B}_2 p^{z_2} & \text{on } (p^*, +\infty), \end{cases}$$

respectively. Here,

$$\begin{bmatrix} \widetilde{B}_1 \\ \widetilde{B}_2 \end{bmatrix} = \begin{bmatrix} p^{*-z_1} & 0 \\ 0 & p^{*-z_2} \end{bmatrix} \begin{bmatrix} \widetilde{a}_{11}p^* + \widetilde{b}_{11} \\ \widetilde{a}_{21}p^* + \widetilde{b}_{21} \end{bmatrix}.$$

Proof. (1) If $\mathcal{S}_i = \emptyset$, we have

$$J_i(p) := \mathbb{E}\left[\int_0^{+\infty} \exp(-rt)(P(t) - C)\mathrm{d}t \middle| X(0) = e_i, P(0) = p\right].$$

In particular, $J_i(0) = -C/r$, but Theorem 4.3.7 tells us that $J_i(0) = -K$ because of $C > rK$. This contradiction leads to $\mathcal{S}_i \neq \emptyset$. In addition, the condition $g_i(0) > \sum_{i=1}^{m} b_{qi} f_q(0)$ in Theorem 4.2.13 reads $-K > -C/r$, i.e., $C > rK$, and we also have $\mathcal{D}_i = (0, C - rK]$. Therefore, by Theorem 4.2.13 and Lemma 4.3.6, it follows that $\mathcal{S}_i = (0, p_i^*]$ for some positive number p_i^*.

(2) `Case 1` $p_1^* < p_2^*$. In this case, by Theorem 4.3.7, we have

$$\begin{cases} J_1(p) = -K \\ J_2(p) = -K \end{cases}$$

on $(0, p_1^*]$,

$$\begin{cases} (r+\lambda_1)J_1(p) - \mu_1 p J_1'(p) - \frac{1}{2}\sigma_1^2 p^2 J_1''(p) - \lambda_1 J_2(p) - p + C = 0 \\ J_2(p) = -K \end{cases} \tag{4.3.6}$$

on $(p_1^*, p_2^*]$, and

$$\begin{cases} (r+\lambda_1)J_1(p) - \mu_1 p J_1'(p) - \frac{1}{2}\sigma_1^2 p^2 J_1''(p) - \lambda_1 J_2(p) - p + C = 0 \\ (r+\lambda_2)J_2(p) - \mu_2 p J_2'(p) - \frac{1}{2}\sigma_2^2 p^2 J_2''(p) - \lambda_2 J_1(p) - p + C = 0 \end{cases} \tag{4.3.7}$$

on $(p_2^*, +\infty)$.

Note that $r+\lambda_1-\mu_1>0$ by Step 2 of the proof of Lemma 4.3.5. We have by (4.3.6)

$$J_1(p)=\frac{p}{r+\lambda_1-\mu_1}-\frac{\lambda_1 K+C}{r+\lambda_1}+A_1p^{y_1}+A_2p^{y_2}\ \text{on}\ (p_1^*,p_2^*],$$

where A_1 and A_2 are two constants, and y_1 and y_2 are the two solutions of the quadratic equation

$$r+\lambda_1-\mu_1 y-\frac{1}{2}\sigma_1^2 y(y-1)=0$$

with $y_1<y_2$.

Since J_1 and J_2 are Lipschitz continuous, we have by (4.3.7)

$$\begin{cases} J_1(p)=\dfrac{(r+\lambda_1+\lambda_2-\mu_2)p}{(r+\lambda_1-\mu_1)(r+\lambda_2-\mu_2)-\lambda_1\lambda_2}-\dfrac{C}{r}+B_1p^{z_1}+B_2p^{z_2} \\ J_2(p)=\dfrac{(r+\lambda_1+\lambda_2-\mu_1)p}{(r+\lambda_1-\mu_1)(r+\lambda_2-\mu_2)-\lambda_1\lambda_2}-\dfrac{C}{r}+\lambda_1^{-1}w_1(z_1)B_1p^{z_1}+ \\ \quad \lambda_1^{-1}w_1(z_2)B_2p^{z_2} \end{cases}$$

on $(p_2^*,+\infty)$, where B_1 and B_2 are some constants, and z_1 and z_2 are the solutions introduced in Lemma 4.3.5.

Therefore, by the C^1 continuity of J_1 and J_2, we have

$$(4.3.8)\qquad \begin{cases} \dfrac{p_1^*}{r+\lambda_1-\mu_1}-\dfrac{\lambda_1K+C}{r+\lambda_1}+A_1p_1^{*y_1}+A_2p_1^{*y_2}=-K \\ \dfrac{1}{r+\lambda_1-\mu_1}+A_1y_1p_1^{*y_1-1}+A_2y_2p_1^{*y_2-1}=0, \end{cases}$$

(4.3.9)
$$\begin{cases} \dfrac{p_2^*}{r+\lambda_1-\mu_1}-\dfrac{\lambda_1K+C}{r+\lambda_1}+A_1p_2^{*y_1}+A_2p_2^{*y_2} \\ \quad =\dfrac{(r+\lambda_1+\lambda_2-\mu_2)p_2^*}{(r+\lambda_1-\mu_1)(r+\lambda_2-\mu_2)-\lambda_1\lambda_2}-\dfrac{C}{r}+B_1p_2^{*z_1}+B_2p_2^{*z_2} \\ \dfrac{1}{r+\lambda_1-\mu_1}+A_1y_1p_2^{*y_1-1}+A_2y_2p_2^{*y_2-1} \\ \quad =\dfrac{r+\lambda_1+\lambda_2-\mu_2}{(r+\lambda_1-\mu_1)(r+\lambda_2-\mu_2)-\lambda_1\lambda_2}+B_1z_1p_2^{*z_1-1}+B_2z_2p_2^{*z_2-1}, \end{cases}$$

and

$$
(4.3.10) \quad \begin{cases} \dfrac{(r+\lambda_1+\lambda_2-\mu_1)p_2^*}{(r+\lambda_1-\mu_1)(r+\lambda_2-\mu_2)-\lambda_1\lambda_2} - \dfrac{C}{r} + \\ \qquad \lambda_1^{-1}w_1(z_1)B_1 p_2^{*z_1} + \lambda_1^{-1}w_1(z_2)B_2 p_2^{*z_2} = -K \\ \dfrac{r+\lambda_1+\lambda_2-\mu_1}{(r+\lambda_1-\mu_1)(r+\lambda_2-\mu_2)-\lambda_1\lambda_2} + \\ \qquad \lambda_1^{-1}w_1(z_1)B_1 z_1 p_2^{*z_1-1} + \lambda_1^{-1}w_1(z_2)B_2 z_2 p_2^{*z_2-1} = 0. \end{cases}
$$

By solving A_1 and A_2 from (4.3.8) and solving A_1 and A_2 from (4.3.9) and (4.3.10), we get

$$
\begin{bmatrix} p_1^{*-y_1} & 0 \\ 0 & p_1^{*-y_2} \end{bmatrix} \begin{bmatrix} a_{11}p_1^* + b_{11} \\ a_{21}p_1^* + b_{21} \end{bmatrix} = \begin{bmatrix} p_2^{*-y_1} & 0 \\ 0 & p_2^{*-y_2} \end{bmatrix} \begin{bmatrix} a_{12}p_2^* + b_{12} \\ a_{22}p_2^* + b_{22} \end{bmatrix}.
$$

Case 2 $p_1^* > p_2^*$. This case is similar to Case 1.

Case 3 $p_1^* = p_2^* =: p^*$. By Theorem 4.3.7, we have

$$
\begin{cases} J_1(p) = -K \\ J_2(p) = -K \end{cases}
$$

on $(0, p^*]$, and

$$
(4.3.11) \quad \begin{cases} (r+\lambda_1)J_1(p) - \mu_1 p J_1'(p) - \dfrac{1}{2}\sigma_1^2 p^2 J_1''(p) - \lambda_1 J_2(p) - p + C = 0 \\ (r+\lambda_2)J_2(p) - \mu_2 p J_2'(p) - \dfrac{1}{2}\sigma_2^2 p^2 J_2''(p) - \lambda_2 J_1(p) - p + C = 0 \end{cases}
$$

on $(p^*, +\infty)$.

Since J_1 and J_2 are Lipschitz continuous, we have by (4.3.11)

$$
\begin{cases} J_1(p) = \dfrac{(r+\lambda_1+\lambda_2-\mu_2)p}{(r+\lambda_1-\mu_1)(r+\lambda_2-\mu_2)-\lambda_1\lambda_2} - \dfrac{C}{r} + \widetilde{B}_1 p^{z_1} + \widetilde{B}_2 p^{z_2} \\ J_2(p) = \dfrac{(r+\lambda_1+\lambda_2-\mu_1)p}{(r+\lambda_1-\mu_1)(r+\lambda_2-\mu_2)-\lambda_1\lambda_2} - \dfrac{C}{r} + \\ \qquad \lambda_1^{-1}w_1(z_1)\widetilde{B}_1 p^{z_1} + \lambda_1^{-1}w_1(z_2)\widetilde{B}_2 p^{z_2} \end{cases}
$$

on $(p^*, +\infty)$, where $\widetilde{B}_1$ and $\widetilde{B}_2$ are some constants, and z_1 and z_2 are the solutions introduced in Lemma 4.3.5.

Therefore, by the C^1 continuity of J_1 and J_2, we have

(4.3.12)
$$\begin{cases} \dfrac{(r+\lambda_1+\lambda_2-\mu_2)p^*}{(r+\lambda_1-\mu_1)(r+\lambda_2-\mu_2)-\lambda_1\lambda_2} - \dfrac{C}{r} + \widetilde{B}_1 p^{*z_1} + \widetilde{B}_2 p^{*z_2} = -K \\ \dfrac{r+\lambda_1+\lambda_2-\mu_2}{(r+\lambda_1-\mu_1)(r+\lambda_2-\mu_2)-\lambda_1\lambda_2} + \widetilde{B}_1 z_1 p^{*z_1-1} + \widetilde{B}_2 z_2 p^{*z_2-1} = 0, \end{cases}$$

and

$$(4.3.13)\quad \begin{cases} \dfrac{(r+\lambda_1+\lambda_2-\mu_1)p^*}{(r+\lambda_1-\mu_1)(r+\lambda_2-\mu_2)-\lambda_1\lambda_2} - \dfrac{C}{r} + \\ \qquad \lambda_1^{-1} w_1(z_1)\widetilde{B}_1 p^{*z_1} + \lambda_1^{-1} w_1(z_2)\widetilde{B}_2 p^{*z_2} = -K \\ \dfrac{r+\lambda_1+\lambda_2-\mu_1}{(r+\lambda_1-\mu_1)(r+\lambda_2-\mu_2)-\lambda_1\lambda_2} + \\ \qquad \lambda_1^{-1} w_1(z_1)\widetilde{B}_1 z_1 p^{*z_1-1} + \lambda_1^{-1} w_1(z_2)\widetilde{B}_2 z_2 p^{*z_2-1} = 0. \end{cases}$$

By solving $\widetilde{B}_1$ and $\widetilde{B}_2$ from (4.3.12) and solving $\widetilde{B}_1$ and $\widetilde{B}_2$ from (4.3.13), we get

$$\begin{bmatrix} \widetilde{a}_{11}p^* + \widetilde{b}_{11} \\ \widetilde{a}_{21}p^* + \widetilde{b}_{21} \end{bmatrix} = \begin{bmatrix} \widetilde{a}_{12}p^* + \widetilde{b}_{12} \\ \widetilde{a}_{22}p^* + \widetilde{b}_{22} \end{bmatrix}.$$

The proof is complete. □

Corollary 4.3.12 *If $r > \mu_2$ and $C > rK$, then the conclusions in Theorem 4.3.11 hold.*

Proof. The proof can be completed by the fact that $r > \mu_2$ implies $r > x_2$. □

Example 4.3.13 Take $\mu_1 = 0.01$, $\mu_2 = 0.10$, $\sigma_1 = \sigma_2 = 0.25$, $r = 0.08$, $\lambda_1 = \lambda_2 = 0.05$, $C = 20$, $K = 5$. Then we have $r = 0.08 > 0.0723 = x_2$ and $C = 20 > 0.40 = rK$. Thus we apply Theorem 4.3.11, and find that ② of Theorem 4.3.11 gives us $(\overline{p}_1^*, \overline{p}_2^*) = (2.08, 1.04)$ and the optimal stopping time $\tau^* = \inf\{t : t > 0, (X(t), P(t)) \in \{e_1\} \times (0, 2.08] \cup \{e_2\} \times (0, 1.04]\}$.

It is interesting to compare regime-switching cases with no regime-switching cases. If there is no regime switching and the price P satisfies

$$\mathrm{d}P(t) = 0.01P(t)\mathrm{d}t + 0.25P(t)\mathrm{d}B(t),$$

the optimal stopping time is $\inf\{t : t > 0, P(t) \in (0, 12.73]\}$. However, if the price P satisfies

$$dP(t) = 0.10P(t)dt + 0.25P(t)dB(t),$$

the firm should never stop the extraction since $r = 0.08 < 0.10$.

In summary, the firm may stop the extraction even though it should never stop the extraction in one of regimes.

4.4 Conclusions

Regime-switching processes were introduced to describe the price of financial assets and commodities[e.g., 10, 12], the stochastic behavior of temperature[21], and so on. Under the assumption that underlying processes are modeled by some regime-switching processes, Guo and Zhang[44] derived an explicit closed solution for perpetual American options, Bae *et al.*[2] investigated dynamic asset allocation among diverse financial markets, and Elias *et al.*[21] valuated temperature-based weather options. These motivate us to study in a uniform way the optimal stopping problems in which underlying processes and payoff functions are modulated by Markov chains.

In this chapter, we employ the viscosity solution technique to analyze optimal stopping problems with regime switching. Specifically, we first prove the value function is a viscosity solution of some variational inequalities; next, we obtain the uniqueness of the viscosity solution of the variational inequalities; then, we study the regularity of the value function and the form of optimal stopping intervals.

In Section 4.3, we provide an application of the results obtained in Section 4.2. At the end of the chapter, a numerical example is demonstrated. From the example, we come to a conclusion that a firm may stop a project even though it should never stop the project in one of regimes.

List of Figures

Bibliography

[1] APPLEBAUM D. Lévy processes and stochastic calculus [M]. 2nd ed. Cambridge: Cambridge University Press, 2009.

[2] BAE G I, KIM W C, MULVEY J M. Dynamic asset allocation for varied financial markets under regime switching framework [J]. European Journal of Operational Research, 2014, 234(2): 450-458.

[3] BAR-ILAN A, STRANGE W C. Investment lags [J]. The American Economic Review, 1996, 86(3): 610-622.

[4] BOLLEN N P B. Real options and product life cycles [J]. Management Science, 1999, 45(5): 670-684.

[5] BOYARCHENKO S, LEVENDORSKIĬ S. Exit problems in regime-switching models [J]. Journal of Mathematical Economics, 2008, 44(2): 180-206.

[6] BOYARCHENKO S, LEVENDORSKIĬ S. Irreversible decisions under uncertainty: optimal stopping made easy [M]. Berlin: Springer-Verlag, 2007.

[7] BREKKE K A, ØKSENDAL B. Optimal switching in an economic activity under uncertainty [J]. SIAM Journal on Control and Optimization, 1994, 32(4): 1021-1036.

[8] BUFFINGTON J, ELLIOTT R J. Regime switching and European options [C]//PASIK-DUNCAN B. Stochastic theory and control. Berlin: Springer-Verlag, 2002: 73-82.

[9] BUFFINGTON J, ELLIOTT R J. American options with regime switch-

ing [J]. International Journal of Theoretical and Applied Finance, 2002, 5(5): 497-514.

[10] CASASSUS J, COLLIN-DUFRESNE P, ROUTLEDGE B R. Equilibrium commodity prices with irreversible investment and non-linear technology [R]. Cambridge, MA: National Bureau of Economic Research, 2005: No. 11864.

[11] CHAN T. Pricing contingent claims on stocks driven by Lévy processes [J]. Annals of Applied Probability, 1999, 9(2): 504-528.

[12] CHERNOV M, GALLANT A R, GHYSELS E, et al. Alternative models for stock price dynamics [J]. Journal of Econometrics, 2003, 116(1/2): 225-257.

[13] CHOI Y K, LEE S W. Investment and abandonment decisions with uncertain price and cost [J]. Journal of Business Finance & Accounting, 2000, 27(1/2): 195-213.

[14] CORCUERA J M, GUERRA J, NUALART D, et al. Optimal investment in a Lévy market [J]. Applied Mathematics and Optimization, 2006, 53(3): 279-309.

[15] COSTENIUC M, SCHNETZER M, TASCHINI L. Entry and exit decision problem with implementation delay [J]. Journal of Applied Probability, 2008, 45(4): 1039-1059.

[16] CRANDALL M G, ISHII H, LIONS P-L. User's guide to viscosity solutions of second order partial differential equations [J]. Bulletin of the American Mathematical Society, 1992, 27(1): 1-67.

[17] D'AURIA B, KELLA O. Markov modulation of a two-sided reflected Brownian motion with application to fluid queues [J]. Stochastic Processes and Their Applications, 2012, 122(4): 1566-1581.

[18] DIXIT A. Entry and exit decisions under uncertainty [J]. Journal of Political Economy, 1989, 97(3): 620-638.

[19] DUCKWORTH J K, ZERVOS M. An investment model with entry and exit decisions [J]. Journal of Applied Probability, 2000, 37(2): 547-559.

[20] EL KAROUI N, LEPELTIER J-P, MARCHAL B. Optimal stopping of controlled Markov processes [C]//FLEMING W H, GOROSTIZA L G. Advances in filtering and optimal stochastic control. Berlin: Springer-

Verlag, 1982: 106-112.

[21] ELIAS R S, WAHAB M I M, FANG L. A comparison of regime-switching temperature modeling approaches for applications in weather derivatives [J]. European Journal of Operational Research, 2014, 232(3): 549-560.

[22] ELOE P, LIU R H, YATSUKI M, et al. Optimal selling rules in a regime-switching exponential Gaussian diffusion model [J]. SIAM Journal on Applied Mathematics, 2008, 69(3): 810-829.

[23] GAUTHIER L, MORELLEC E. Investment under uncertainty with implementation delay [DB/OL]. (2000-03-08)[2016-03-01]. https://infoscience.epfl.ch/record/188140/files/morellec_delay.PDF.

[24] GUO X, ZHANG Q. Optimal selling rules in a regime switching model [J]. IEEE Transactions on Automatic Control, 2005, 50(9): 1450-1455.

[25] GUO X. An explicit solution to an optimal stopping problem with regime switching [J]. Journal of Applied Probability, 2001, 38(2): 464-481.

[26] HAINAUT D. Entry and exit decisions with switching regime cash flows [J]. International Journal of Managerial Finance, 2012, 8(1): 58-72.

[27] JOHNSON T C, ZERVOS M. The explicit solution to a sequential switching problem with non-smooth data [J]. Stochastics an International Journal of Probability and Stochastics Processes, 2010, 82(1): 69-109.

[28] KARATZAS I, SHREVE S E. Brownian motion and stochastic calculus [M]. 2nd ed. New York: Springer-Verlag, 1991.

[29] KLEBANER F C. Introduction to stochastic calculus with applications [M]. London: Imperial College Press, 1998.

[30] KONGSTED H C. Entry and exit decisions under uncertainty: the limiting deterministic case [J]. Economics Letters, 1996, 51(1): 77-82.

[31] LEVENDORSKIĬ S. Perpetual American options and real options under mean-reverting processes [DB/OL]. (2005-05-04)[2016-03-01]. http://ssrn.com/abstract=714321 or http://dx.doi.org/10.2139/ssrn.714321.

[32] MEDVEGYEV P. Stochastic integration theory [M]. Oxford: Oxford University Press, 2007.

[33] MORDECKI E. Optimal stopping and perpetual options for Lévy processes [J]. Finance and Stochastics, 2002, 6(4): 473-493.

[34] ØKSENDAL B. Optimal stopping with delayed information [J]. Stochas-

tics and Dynamics, 2005, 5(2): 271-280.

[35] ØKSENDAL B, SULEM A. Applied stochastic control of jump diffusions [M]. 2nd ed. Berlin: Springer-Verlag, 2007.

[36] PHAM H. Continuous-time stochastic control and optimization with financial applications [M]. Berlin: Springer-Verlag, 2009.

[37] PINDYCK R S. Investments of uncertain cost [J]. Journal of Financial Economics, 1993, 34(1): 53-76.

[38] PROTTER P E. Stochastic integration and differential equations [M]. 2nd ed. Berlin: Springer-Verlag, 2005.

[39] SEIERSTAD A. Stochastic control in discrete and continuous time [M]. New York: Springer-Verlag, 2009.

[40] SHIRAKAWA H. Evaluation of investment opportunity under entry and exit decisions [C]//MARUYAMA T. Mathematical analysis in economics. Kyoto: Research Institute for Mathematical Sciences, 1997: 107-124.

[41] SØDAL S. Entry and exit decisions based on a discount factor approach [J]. Journal of Economic Dynamics and Control, 2006, 30(11): 1963-1986.

[42] TOUZI N. Optimal stochastic control, stochastic target problems, and backward SDE [M]. New York: Springer-Verlag, 2013.

[43] TSEKREKOS A E. The effect of mean reversion on entry and exit decisions under uncertainty [J]. Journal of Economic Dynamics and Control, 2010, 34(4): 725-742.

[44] ZHANG Q, GUO X. Closed-form solutions for perpetual American put options with regime switching [J]. SIAM Journal on Applied Mathematics, 2004, 64(6): 2034-2049.

[45] ZHANG Y-C. On some mathematical problems from asset pricing [D]. Tianjin: Nankai University, 2013.

[46] ZHANG Y-C. Entry and exit decisions with linear costs under uncertainty [J]. Stochastics an International Journal of Probability and Stochastic Processes, 2015, 87(2): 209-234.

[47] ZHANG Y-C. Entry-exit decisions with implementation delay under uncertainty [DB/OL]. (2015-11-30)[2016-03-01]. http://arxiv.org/pdf/1503.01285v2.pdf.

[48] ZHANG Y-C. Entry-exit decisions with underlying processes following

geometric Lévy processes [Z]. Preprint, 2015.

[49] ZHANG Y-C, Zhang N. Optimal stopping problems with regime switching: a viscosity solution method [DB/OL]. (2015-12-24)[2016-03-01]. http://arxiv.org/pdf/1404.3372v3.pdf.

[50] ZHANG Z-S. Lecture on differential topology (in Chinese) [M]. Beijing: Peking University Press, 1996.